p.48 - it is easier to see the lack of
wisdom in someone else's choice than
to make a sensible one yourself

Gardening for Love

17
P. 18
24
35, 36, 37
39
42, 43
44
+ 79

Japanese Climbing fern (45)

Scilla hyacinthoides
7. Ginger Lily (p.43)

Clematis crispa (116)

Gardening for Love

THE MARKET BULLETINS

by Elizabeth Lawrence

Edited, with an introduction by Allen Lacy

Duke University Press   Durham 1987

Third printing

The chapter ornaments were drawn by Abigail Rorer.
They are, in order of appearance, *Sedum sarmentosum,*
Malva moschata, Malvaviscus drummondii, Malva moschata,
Zephyranthes atamasco, Habenaria ciliaris, Viola fimbriatula,
Sedum sarmentosum.

Library of Congress Cataloging-in-Publication Data
Lawrence, Elizabeth.
Gardening for love.
Bibliography: p.
Includes index.
1. Plants, Ornamental—Southern States—Seeds—
Marketing—Periodicals. 2. Flowers—Southern States—
Seeds—marketing—Periodicals. 3. Plants, Ornamental—
Southern States—Marketing—Periodicals. 4. Flowers—
Southern States—marketing—Periodicals. 5. Plants,
Ornamental—Southern States. 6. Flowers—Southern
States. 7. Horticultural literature—Southern States.
8. Marketing literature—Southern States. I. Lacy,
Allen, 1935–   . II. Title.
SB406.65s85L38   1987   635'.0975   86-32896

To Hannah Withers and all my gardening friends

Contents

The love of gardening is a seed that once sown never dies.
—Gertrude Jekyll

Introduction

I never knew Miss Elizabeth Lawrence, and feel the poorer for it. Our affections ran deep for some of the same things: gardening and its rich literature from Virgil to the present, the mountains and piedmont and coastal plains of North Carolina, and the sound of a postman coming up the walk with a package of plants or a good long letter from a plant-loving friend in a faraway state. Elizabeth Lawrence loved not only to garden, but also to write about gardening, and at her death in the early summer of 1985, she left those of us who like to read about gardening a rich legacy of books, true gardening classics which will be read for generations. *A Southern Garden, Gardens in Winter, The Little Bulbs*—these will continue to find and delight new readers. Among books on gardening, they are hardy perennials that have already taken their place alongside Alice Morse Earle's *Old Time Gardens* (1901) and Louise Beebe Wilder's *Adventures with Hardy Bulbs* (1936), to name just two of several books Miss Lawrence treasured and constantly quoted.

At the moment, Elizabeth Lawrence is known primarily as a regional garden writer, specifically a southern one. This reputation is apt in part, but it also misses the mark. First, all garden writers are not alike. Some deal —and usefully so—mainly in how-to and when-to, in practical matters. Others are writers first and garden writers second. This kind of garden writer is extremely close to the poet and the novelist, as the novelist Beverly Lowry has recently pointed out: there is a consistent voice to be heard, a sense of character and of story, as well as practical information about plants. Elizabeth Lawrence is just such a garden writer, and among the very best of the kind. Second, "regional writer" has undeserved overtones of something second-rate. All writers are regional; they must live in some particular place, and die in some particular place, even if the places aren't the same. This truth applies especially to those who write on gardening. Anyone who both gardens and writes about gardening must inevitably do so in some particular spot, with its peculiarities of soil and weather and its long lists of plants that find that spot congenial and its equally long list of plants that do not. All garden writers are thus regional ones—even *local* ones, a fact sometimes forgotten by critics. The British writers William Robinson, Gertrude Jekyll, and Vita Sackville-West have been extremely influential on both sides of the Atlantic, yet there is much in their writing that is parochial, in the best sense of the word. Elizabeth Lawrence understood this point very well indeed. Her assessment of Miss Jekyll, in the introduction she wrote in 1957 to an anthology just reprinted by David Godine under the title *The Essential Gertrude Jekyll*, was called "Miss Jekyll of Munstead Wood." Had she been asked to write a similar introduction to an anthology of Sackville-West's writings, she probably would have called it "Miss Sackville-West of Sissinghurst Castle, Kent." The true gardener, since Eden, has been rooted in the same patch of earth as the plants that grow there. To think of Elizabeth Lawrence as a regional writer, but not to think of Jekyll or Sackville-West under the same rubric, is pure bias that somehow treats British garden writing as universal in application, in distinction to garden writing that originates elsewhere. It is worth mentioning, incidentally, that Miss Lawrence's books have been well received in Great Britain, by gardeners and horticulturists who have ordered them from American booksellers.

The same bias—northeastern rather than British—can also be found in our own country and its ways of classifying garden writers. Katharine S. White gardened in Maine. Eleanor Perènyi tends her garden in coastal Connecticut. White's *Onward and Upward in the Garden* and Perènyi's *Green Thoughts: A Writer in the Garden* have rightfully been called American garden classics; they have not, however, been called New England gardening classics. That's what they are, of course, but they also transcend the category, because of their sense of history and their awareness of other places, other times, and that's my point. Elizabeth Lawrence was a southern garden writer (meaning that she took a primary but by no means exclusive interest in the South—a region with great diversities of climate, soil, and flora), but she also transcended the category. She was keenly aware of the activities of gardeners all over the country, through travel and through correspondence, including correspondence with gardeners in the North and in the West. Perhaps one day someone will study her long correspondence with Katharine S. White — and with Grace Root of Clinton, New York, a magnificent gardener and a canny one, who, by setting up a complicated trust fund and a foundation, managed the difficult trick of making sure that the garden she made over a lifetime would survive her for generations to come.

*

Now comes *Gardening for Love*, a new, but posthumous, book by Elizabeth Lawrence, something of whose origins I must now relate.

As Miss Lawrence explains it, sometime after World War II, Eudora Welty put her name on the mailing list of the *Mississippi Market Bulletin*, a periodical published twice a month in Jackson under state subsidy and sent out free to all who asked. This bulletin consisted entirely of classified advertisements, free of charge to the farmers of the state who had land and livestock and produce to offer — and to their wives, who often had plants and seeds to sell for pin money. Elizabeth Lawrence was thus introduced not only to the bulletin but also to a passion which absorbed her the rest of her life. She ordered plants and seeds through the mail, usually with a question or two for the person who sold them. Letters flew back and forth between Charlotte, North Carolina, and places like Crystal Springs, Mississippi. In due course, Lawrence discovered similar market bulletins published in other states, almost exclusively in the South, and also private newsletters, such as *Joe's Bulletin*, almost exclusively in the North, in which small growers all over the country could advertise their plants to other gardeners. Elizabeth Lawrence subscribed to them all, and kept the mailman busy with her letters ordering plants and asking questions about their culture, their common names, and their lore. She carried on an extensive parallel correspondence with botanists and horticultural authorities, seeking scientific identifications of the plants she got through the mail, often plants which were either rare or not available commercially from large growers and nurseries. She was fascinated by the common names of these plants—their "sweet and country names, some of them going back to Shakespeare and the Bible." But she also wanted their precise taxonomy, their botanical names according to the Linnean system of binomial classification.

At some point before 1962, Miss Lawrence began to write *Gardening for Love*, a manuscript which described the bulletins, the plants she found there, and the letters she received. She continued to write until 1978 or thereabouts, when she apparently put the book aside, hoping to finish it one day and being encouraged by family and friends to do so. The task was impossible. The book ranged widely into the whole history of gardening in the Western world, with references to Pliny and Virgil, to herbalists such as Parkinson and Gerard, and to more recent writers such as Thoreau and Sarah Orne Jewett— and to Eudora Welty. Miss Lawrence was in failing health. Equally disturbing, the periodicals that were Lawrence's subject were declining in number and altering their character. The private newsletters like *Joe's Bulletin* and *Ozark Gardens* went out of business. Today Alabama, Florida, Georgia, Kentucky, Mississippi, North Carolina, and West Virginia still publish bulletins. The Georgia *Farmers and Consumers Market Bulletin* seems especially healthy, having been featured in September 1986 in both the *New York Times* and on the NBC "Today" show. But I subscribe to several of the remaining bulletins, and they have lost some of the flavor Miss Lawrence relished so much. The "sweet country names" are uncommon now, and many of the plants advertised are the same named cultivars of irises and daylilies that are sold by large mail-order nurseries. *Gardening for Love*, however, captures the spirit of the market bulletins at their height, at a time when, as Dudley Clendinen put it in his story in the *New York Times*, "for countless rural families there were just three printed references in the house: the Bible, the Market Bulletin, and *The Saturday Evening Post*."

In 1984, thanks to the providential intervention of Miss Lawrence's friend of many decades, William Lanier Hunt, the material for *Gardening for Love* was packed into a huge pasteboard box and shipped to Joanne Ferguson, editor in chief of the Duke University Press (which had already arranged to reprint Lawrence's *The Little Bulbs*), for safe-keeping and for possible publication, if a willing editor could be found. I was that willing editor. The pasteboard box came into my life in late April of 1985, shortly before Elizabeth Lawrence's death. I was visiting friends in Durham when Joanne Ferguson asked me to examine the contents of the box. Some things had been sorted out in rough fashion, but its contents were varied, to put it mildly. There were hundreds of letters to Lawrence, from people in many walks of life. All touched on gardening or the market bulletins, and on many other things as well. Letters from the same persons were clipped together. Sometimes they spanned a decade or more, tracing out not only the love for plants but also the stuff of life—the deaths of spouses or of children, the onset of serious illness, the loneliness of elderly women for whom writing letters to Miss Lawrence was obviously a lifeline. In the box, there were packages of seed. There were some of her newspaper columns. There were several hundred pages of text, poorly typed by someone other than Miss Lawrence (who never learned to type), on an old manual typewriter that had seen better days and that seldom got a fresh ribbon. There were a few—very few—pages written by her, in the tiny, almost illegible hand that was the despair of many of her friends. On one page she toyed with a table of contents and with a title, considering The Brothers of the Spade but then rejecting it for the present title. There were market bulletins aplenty and yellowed copies of Ozark Gardens, Joe's Bulletin, and The Garden Gate, some of these mimeographed, some printed on cheap pulp paper already beginning to crumble.

Joanne Ferguson asked two questions of me. As someone who had had editorial experiences with university presses and also as a free-lance gardening writer, did I think the box had a book in it? And if so, would I agree to conjure it up? I read perhaps fifty pages, mostly from the essay on the Mississippi bulletin. Conjure up a book? The phrase was apt, for there was magic in that box —good clean prose that sang and spoke from the heart. There was Miss Lawrence's almost Homeric joy in making lists: lists of wonderful local names for plants, names sometimes going back to Chaucer's time but still used in the rural South in the middle of the twentieth century, names taken over from American Indians, names not found in seed catalogs or gardening encyclopedias; lists of herbal remedies and the ills they were said to cure; and even lists of the sorts of hound dogs used and sold and traded in Mississippi. There was no way that I could even consider refusing to edit this book.

*

Editing takes many forms. It may be the kind of monumental revision Maxwell Perkins undertook in turning
Thomas Wolfe's sprawling manuscript into *Look Homeward
Angel*. It may be something much simpler, a matter of
checking for consistency of style and internal logic. Ideally,
it is something that takes place between a writer and an
editor, a transaction between two people who have in
common the desire to publish the best book possible.
This ideal is obviously not possible to realize in a posthumous book, for the editor must answer the same questions he asks about a manuscript, guided by common
sense and a respect for the personal voice of the writer. I
hope and pray that Lawrence would approve of the way I
have edited her manuscript, but at the same time I must
point out that in its present form *Gardening for Love* embod-
ies a good bit of editorial judgment, for that pasteboard
box much resembled a box containing the pieces of
several jigsaw puzzles, some of them incomplete, dumped
together. The pages were unnumbered, with many missing or out-of-sequence. Some material existed in multi-
ple versions, with no way of determining which version
she would have preferred. Some mysteries could not be
solved. Miss Edna Bestard of Eureka Springs, Arkansas,
stopped publishing *Ozark Gardens* in 1962, a fact Lawrence
must have known. Her essay about this periodical, which
treats it as a flourishing concern, must therefore have
been written prior to its demise. She surely would have
revised the essay herself, and I was tempted to do it for
her by changing tenses and trying to write in her voice a
paragraph of introduction. I resisted the temptation, letting some of the mystery remain.

But if one responsibility of an editor is respect for the

writer, an equal one is concern for the reader, and I admit to making a number of changes in the text. Botanical nomenclature is a restless affair, old names being altered as older ones are found or as the understanding of the relations among different species and genera of plants change. With a great deal of assistance from Nancy Goodwin of Montrose Nursery in Hillsborough and Edith Eddleman, the curator of the remarkable perennial border at the North Carolina State University Arboretum in Raleigh, two good friends of mine who match Elizabeth Lawrence in both their love of plants and their insistence on precise identification, I have brought scientific names up to date, sometimes giving the older names as well, since they often are still used in the nursery trade. I have also tried to identify, at their first mention, the persons whose names appear in the text, so that the reader will know that "Mrs. Harmon" is one of Lawrence's correspondents who lived in Saluda, South Carolina, and that "Mrs. Ballard" is Ernesta Drinker Ballard, a prominent horticulturist from Pennsylvania whose book on houseplants Lawrence much admired. I have also omitted some material that Lawrence might have included, trying to keep as far as possible to the subject of the market bulletins. (There was considerable temptation to include her booklet, Lob's Wood, a sequel to The Little Bulbs, and a further account of her friend Carl Krippendorf's vast woodland garden east of Cincinnati, which has been privately printed by the nature center established there after his death, but I was finally persuaded that its inclusion would create a disunified and imbalanced book.) I did, however, include a few pages on the Chinaberry tree, though it was not a market bulletin item. Finally, again with the help of Nancy Goodwin and Edith Eddleman, I have occasionally added a commercial source for a plant mentioned in the text.

Readers of *Gardening for Love* will share, I feel sure, the admiration that I feel for Elizabeth Lawrence's vast knowledge of plants, her feeling for language, and her personal voice, which was at once human and humane. They will also admire the people like Kim Kimery and Ethel Harmon, whose letters to her are so frequently quoted in the text. But some of the enormous pleasure I have found in editing this book cannot be passed on to readers, except indirectly. A pasteboard box full of old papers? It could contain anything—tax returns, newspaper clippings, personal letters of no special character, things to be thrown away before the garage sale. The pasteboard box I inherited was a treasure, of course, because it contained the manuscript of Elizabeth Lawrence. But equally wonderful, the box was full of other voices. Miss Lawrence's own manuscript may have been in disarray, stuffed into the box, in the way that many writers have of treating their own drafts and re-drafts. The letters she received in connection with her long project of writing a book on the market bulletins, however, were lovingly treated, letters from each correspondent stapled or clipped together, usually in chronological order, as has already been mentioned. The earliest letters are dated 1944, the latest 1982. Some of Miss Lawrence's correspondents were highly educated, able to speak knowingly about chromosome counts or the poetry of Baudelaire. Others had only a grade-school education in a one-room country school, but were nevertheless able to write precisely and often poetically about the plants they raised and the lives they lived, both the griefs and the joys they knew. In many of

these letters, one finds the evidences of the southern
social history of which Lawrence spoke in her essay on
the Mississippi bulletin. Almost at random, I select the
following paragraph from a letter to her in the late 1970s,
which in personal terms tells the story of the farm crisis
of the 1980s and the crisis of aging in all times and places.
"I have about twenty acres rented to gov and about 20
acres in soy beans rented to a neighbor for we don't have
help to farm. And it is about out of the question now to
hire anyone to do any thing. We have let everything go
for past 12 years after my husband's health failed him,
and now the buildings are falling down and I just have to
look at them. I am tempted when the weather gets better
to get a hammer and start tearing them down. I am sending you the daffodil Moshatu and Roman hyacinths later
and then when shooting star comes out I will send it."
The theme may be gardening and plants, but life has a
way of intruding, and the people who wrote Elizabeth
Lawrence told her all about it.

*

Elizabeth Lawrence was born in Marietta, Georgia, on
May 27, 1904, the first of two daughters of Samuel
Lawrence, an engineer educated at Georgia Tech, and
Elizabeth Bradenbaugh Lawrence. She spent most of her
childhood in the hamlet of Garysburg, North Carolina,
where her father owned and operated a quarry. In a brief
autobiography published in the 1943 issue of *Herbertia*
accompanying her article "Amaryllids in a Southern
Garden," just after the Amaryllis Society had honored
her with its Herbert Award, she recalls her earliest introduction to the pleasures of gardening and to its connection with other human goods.

When I was a little girl, my mother took great pains to interest me in learning to know the birds and wild flowers and in planting a garden. I thought that roots and bulbs and seeds were as wonderful as flowers, and the Latin names on seed packages as full of enchantment as the counting-out rhymes that children chant in the spring. I remember the first time I planted seeds. My mother asked me if I knew the Parable of the Sower. I said I did not, and she took me into the house and read it to me. Once the relation between poetry and the soil is established in the mind, all growing things are endowed with more than material beauty.

In Miss Lawrence's twelfth year, her family moved to Raleigh, North Carolina, to a huge frame house on Hillsborough Street (now a fraternity house in a tired and run-down neighborhood) with a commodious front porch and an already established garden.

It was fall when we came, and there was not much in bloom—only some old fashioned roses and chrysanthemums that the frost had not caught. But that first spring was like living my favorite book, *The Secret Garden*. Every day the leaves and flower buds of some plant that we did not know was there would break through the cold earth. There were snowdrops under the hedge, and crocuses in the grass, and the garden pattern was picked out in daffodils. And under the eaves of the summer house a single fat white hyacinth bloomed. No other spring has ever been so beautiful, except the spring of the year I came home from college. That first spring in the South after four years in New York led me to choose gardening as a profession.

Those four years in New York were spent at Barnard College, where she majored in English, acquiring her knowledge and love of English poetry and of the Greek and Roman classics that were always present in her writing about gardening. After her return to Raleigh, she began to master the botanical and horticultural knowledge that were necessary for her to garden well professionally.

In the fall, a course in Landscape Architecture (the first in the South) was started at North Carolina State College, and I started with it, the only girl in the class. One morning a visitor came into the drafting room and stopped at my drawing table in passing, and said, "I know another Miss Lawrence who is a landscape architect. She knows as much about plant material as any one in the profession." I felt as if the mantle of the other Miss Lawrence had been thrown across my shoulders. I had never heard of her before, and I have never heard of her since, but because of her I felt a compulsion to study plants. I soon learned, however, that a knowledge of plant material for the South could not be got in the library, most of the literature of gardening being for a different climate, and that I would have to grow the plants in my garden and learn about them for myself.

Miss Lawrence's remarks should not be taken, however, as a rejection of books, considering that she wrote several based both on her own experiences and those of other gardeners and on the literature of gardening. Her judg-

Lawrence in her Raleigh garden

ment in the introduction to *A Southern Garden* (1942) on those who praise "dirt" gardening was telling: "When a gardener has identified himself as the dirt variety he feels a marked superiority. But dirty fingernails are not the only requirement for growing plants. One must be as willing to study as to dig, for a knowledge of plants is acquired as much from books as from experience."

The autobiographical remarks in that issue of *Herbertia* are rare, for Elizabeth Lawrence had very little to say about herself for publication. She wrote in the first person, but she wrote about her experience with plants and about the experience of her many friends with plants, saying little about her life, not even about her travel in Great Britain in the 1920s and then again in her later years, with her friend Hannah Withers. The remarks of Elisabeth

Lawrence in her Charlotte garden

Woodburn, one of the first readers of the edited manuscript of *Gardening for Love*, are apt: "Throughout she shows a real appreciation for others as revealed by their actions, their letters, and their seed and plant offerings. Miss Lawrence is obviously one who recognizes genuine worth in others without feeling the need to prove who she is by a single word of deprecation or hint of superiority. It shows a rare sensitivity."

I have only the barest of outlines of Lawrence's biography. She moved with her mother, widowed since 1935, to a house on Ridgewood Avenue in Charlotte, North Carolina, in 1950. Her sister lived next door with her own family, including a nephew and a niece Miss Lawrence adored, even if she did sometimes say the nephew was her greatest failure, since she couldn't interest him in plants in the slightest. It must have been shortly after she moved to Charlotte that her interest in the market bulletins was awakened by Eudora Welty and that her years of correspondence with gardeners throughout the rural South began. She published *The Little Bulbs* in 1957, *Gardens in Winter* in 1961. In 1959 she became the Sunday garden columnist for the *Charlotte Observer*, continuing to write the column until 1975. Her first column, with an accompanying photograph showing her standing on a brick path behind a wrought-iron gate half-ajar, began: "This is the gate of my garden. I invite you to enter it, not only into my garden, but into the world of gardens—a world as old as the history of man, and as new as the latest contributions of science; a world of mystery, adventure, and romance; a world of poetry and philoso-

phy; a world of beauty; and a world of work. Never let yourself be deceived about the work. There is no royal road to learning (as my grandmother used to say). And there is no royal road to gardening—although men seem to think that there is." Lawrence then went on to chide her editor for telling her that labor-saving devices have taken the hard work out of gardening. She found this notion a piece of nonsense, and at the end of her column stated the plain truth she knew: "Any garden demands as much of its maker as he has to give. But I do not need to tell you, if you are a gardener, that no other undertaking will give as great a return for the amount of effort put into it."

Plain truths, stated forthrightly and sometimes a little testily to editors who didn't understand them, were one of Miss Lawrence's strong suits. Among the papers in that pasteboard box I found a letter from a magazine editor asking her about her "notable affinities and aversions in vocational and avocational fields." Her reply is worth preserving here: "Don't know what this means, but for the record: I design gardens but cannot bear to be called a Landscape Architect; lecture and write about gardening, but cannot bear to be called an expert. Cannot bear to be called an amateur, but like to be taken seriously as a gardener and a writer. (Am taken seriously as a lecturer—anybody is). Cannot bear for people to say (as they often do) that I am better at plant material than design: I cannot help it if I have to use my own well-designed garden as a laboratory, thereby ruining it as a garden."

Elizabeth Lawrence was in failing health in her last few years. In October, 1984, she moved to a nursing home in

Edgewater, Maryland, near her niece, Elizabeth Rogers, in Annapolis. She died of heart failure on June 11, 1985, and was buried in the churchyard of St. James Episcopal Church in Lothian, Maryland. There was a memorial service for her in Marietta, Georgia, at a Lawrence family reunion five days after her death, on the same day that a long obituary in the *Charlotte Observer* quoted her friend and physician Dr. W. B. Mayer, who observed that she was "the Jane Austen of the gardening literary world."

*

I have been the editor of Miss Lawrence's *Gardening for Love*, not her biographer. But after an article about her new book appeared in the *Charlotte Observer* several months in advance of the book's appearance, I heard from a great many of her friends all over the South, saying how dearly they had loved their "Libba" (as those close to her called her), and how eager they were for this final testimony from her. The calls and letters I received were touching, and it seems appropriate to let the last word belong to one of her gardening friends, Mrs. Mary O. Shorrock of Lake Placid, Florida, who has graciously given her permission to publish her personal letter of August 21, 1986.

Dear Dr. Lacy:

I received a clipping from the *Charlotte Observer* today, sent to me from a friend who knew that when I lived in Charlotte nearly twenty years ago, Elizabeth Lawrence was a very dear friend.

I am so very glad that someone is editing her book. The last letter that I got from Elizabeth several years ago was one in which she advised me to advertize in the Florida farmers bulletin to find a start of a particular plant that I had been unable to find at a nursery. Every time we walked in her yard, she could remember from which bulletin she had received each plant. She could remember its history and its original owner's personality. Today my sister in northern Alabama has scions from plants that I received originally from Elizabeth.

In Charlotte, my yard abutted a woodland that was rich with North Carolina wildflowers. Elizabeth, another of her friends, and I used to get down on our hands and knees crawling through the thick covering of fallen leaves to discover the very earliest of wildflowers. She had a beautiful garden and loved to share her plants with a fellow gardener. She knew where the rare nurseries with unusual plants and rock garden perennials were to be found—and she loved sharing that information.

I have spent many afternoons (raw wet ones) in front of a roaring fire in her house, talking about plants—and human beings, because she nurtured the people that she loved just as she nurtured her plants.

She is a part of my life's growth, and added a great depth to my life while I was in Charlotte. In those three short years, she had so much influence on my gardening enthusiasm, more than anyone else I have known. She made me so very aware of wildflowers that I have done a great deal of study on them in these sand flats of Florida, where everything is so completely different from our Charlotte area. Yet when I sent her a scrap book of the year's wildflower bloom in my area of Florida, she was able to identify plants that I thought native to the Florida Ridge as plants that Dr. Heckenbleikner had taken her to see in the N.C. sandy coastline area.

Please let me know when her book is ready for market. I would like very much to have another concrete bit of Elizabeth to hold in my hands, as I hold the memories that I have of her in my heart.

Thank you,

Mary O. Shorrock

*

Acknowledgments. In the course of editing this book, I have incurred some debts, which must be acknowledged here. My debt to Joanne Ferguson is obviously immense. I owe thanks to the Research and Professional Development Committee of Stockton State College for a grant making it possible to devote an entire summer to the task at hand. I would also like to thank Phyllis Ahlsted, Christal Springer, and Robert Vaughn of the Stockton College Library for technical assistance. Miss Lawrence's nephew, Warren Way III, and her niece, Elizabeth Rogers, have been extremely helpful and supportive in many ways, as has Carol Wells, the librarian at Northwestern Louisiana State University who has cataloged the archives there containing much of Lawrence's correspondence. Betsy Asplundh, an intern at the Duke Press, has been extremely resourceful in researching the Bibliography. I have already expressed gratitude to Nancy Goodwin and to Edith Eddleman for assisting with botanical names. I am also indebted to Professor J. C. Raulston of The North Carolina State University Arboretum, where many of the plants that Lawrence grew in her garden in Raleigh have found a permanent home. To many of Miss Lawrence's friends, but especially Hannah Withers, Dannye Romine, John Jamison, Sarah Hodges and Mary O. Shorrock, I am grateful for the reminiscences they have shared and the encouragement they have given.

Allen Lacy
Linwood, New Jersey
September 1986

Preface: "A Friendly Society"

Ever since the Second World War, I have been in correspondence with the country gardeners who advertise their flowers in the southern market bulletins, and who garden for love. Their love shines out in the mere listing of the names of the flowers. These hard-working women, who always find time to answer letters from other gardeners, belong to that great fraternity, The Brothers of the Spade. In 1735, Peter Collinson of London wrote John Custis of Williamsburg,

> I think there is no Greater pleasure than to be Communicative and oblige others. It is laying an obligation and I seldome fail of Returns for Wee Brothers of the Spade find it very necessary to share amongst us the seeds that come annually from Abroad. It not only preserves a Friendly Society but secures our Collections, for if one does not raise a seed perhaps another does & if one Looses a plant another can Supply him. By this Means our Gardens are wonder-

fully Improved in Variety to what they was Twenty
Years agon.

Plants that traveled from London to Williamsburg, and
from Williamsburg to London and then to other parts of
the world, still appear on the market bulletin lists, and
still go on from garden to garden: fringe tree, cucumber
tree, sweet gum, and sassafras; sweet-smelling melons
and grapes; chinquapins and "ivy," as kalmia is still called
by some in the southern mountains. And the farm
women are as communicative and obliging as the two
eighteenth-century gentlemen on either side of the
Atlantic. A question and a stamped envelope bring a
warm response, a flood of information, an outpouring
from the heart, and often—as the market bulletins are
published primarily in the Bible Belt—a religious tract or
a request for your prayers.

These old ladies—and an occasional gentleman—who
sell flowers through the mail are amateurs in the true
sense of the word: they garden for love. And their love is
a saving love. Among them they keep in cultivation many
valuable plants that would otherwise be lost, and they
preserve a reservoir of stock material that could never be
collected in any one place, even an institution. Preservation of plant material depends upon individual effort,
and it is only in private gardens, in lonely farm yards, or
around deserted houses that certain plants, long out of
commerce, are still to be found.

Gardeners are generous because nature is generous to
them, and because they know what it means to read
about something and not to be able to get it. To the
Brothers of the Spade, a rare plant is above the price of

rubies. "If you had sent me 20 times the weight of the seeds in gold it would not have bin the 20eth part so acceptable," John Custis wrote Peter Collinson to thank him for stones of a "Double Blossome peach which at the time of flowering is a most beautiful sight." In *The American Gardener*, William Cobbett said he preferred a fine carnation to a gold watch studded with diamonds. E. A. Bowles, in *A Handbook of Crocus and Colchicums*, said he would rather have been the raiser of *Colchicum speciosum album* than the owner of a Derby winner, and I am sure that Mr. Bowles meant it.

Those who follow the market bulletins also garden for love, and they are members of the Friendly Society of Inveterate Letter Writers. Eudora Welty introduced me to some of these delightful people. Then I found the Dormans, Caroline and her sister-in-law Ruth. Ruth lived in the country near Shreveport, and Caroline lived at Briarwood in a log cabin in a forest in northern Louisiana, where she grew wildflowers and painted them and also grew everything else she could get her hands on. Because of the market bulletins, I have written many a letter, and gotten many a letter in return, from people like the Dormans, from professional botanists such as Dr. B. Y. Morrison, head of the USDA Department of Plant Exploration and Introduction, and Dr. Frederick Meyer, botanist at the National Arboretum, and from plant-lovers such as Kim Kimery and Weezie Smith and Ethel Harmon. I treasure these letters, have kept them, and have much drawn on them in this book, as is, I hope, obvious.

In writing about the bulletins I have put the Mississippi bulletin first, because I had been reading it for several years before the Dormans told me that Louisiana,

Alabama, and Florida also put out bulletins. Then I began writing to the departments of agriculture of states along the Eastern Seaboard, discovering that these bulletins are largely a southern institution. In a news sheet of classified advertisements called *The Garden Gate*, I found that R. L. ("Anzio Bob") Shreiber would supply the addresses of ten free market bulletins for a dollar and a stamped envelope. I complied, and he wrote:

> Dear E.L.,
>
> I see you already know 7 of the 10 bulletins, also the North Carolina bulletin, which is not sent to persons outside of North Carolina. I think they are making a mistake as I have bought hundreds of dollars of plants from other state bulletins. In addition to those you already receive you will find Kentucky, West Virginia, and Tennessee on my list. The following states do not issue a bulletin: Illinois, Missouri, Texas, Oklahoma, Kansas, Wisconsin, and Michigan. I wrote to Iowa, but did not receive an answer. I eventually expect to contact every state in the U.S. including Alaska and Hawaii. If I learn of any more free bulletins, you are entitled to receive their names, as you are on my mailing list for gardening information. Thanking you for the $ and hoping you get a $'s worth, I beg to remain,
>
> > Very Cordially Yours,
> > Anzio Bob
> > (R. L. Shreiber)

I did feel I had my dollar's worth, but I heard no more from Anzio Bob, and after adding Virginia to my list and finding no bulletins from the West Coast, I think I have found them all, as well as a few privately owned bulletins for small advertisers whose states do not offer them the means of selling their plants to other gardeners across the land.

*

Louisiana, South Carolina, and Georgia were the first states to publish market bulletins. On July 14, 1966, the *Louisiana Weekly Market Bulletin* celebrated the fiftieth anniversary of a publication that had started out as a mimeographed sheet. Two weeks later, William Harrelson, South Carolina's commissioner of agriculture, paid tribute to the Louisiana bulletin's anniversary, at the same time noting that "Your *South Carolina Market Bulletin* also is rich in more than half a century of service." Mr. Harrelson wrote further that "the original idea of a market bulletin for South Carolina came in the summer of 1913 when Col. E. J. Watson, Commissioner of Agriculture, proposed the establishment of a State Bureau of Marketing." The first weekly market bulletin was published in sheet form on September 10, 1917. The bulletin has long been a splendid way for people wishing to buy plants to get together with those wishing to sell them. In 1968 and 1969, it published some 17,615 advertisements, of which 2,462 were either "Plants and Flowers" or "Garden Plants," meaning such things as strawberries and blueberries, asparagus and collards, chinquapins and scuppernongs.

In 1961, the Louisiana commissioner of agriculture, Dave L. Pearce, wrote me proudly about his state's market bulletin: "At the present time, we send out about 133,000 each week, which go to every state in the United States. . . . Today's Market Bulletin still reflects the agricultural economy of Louisiana—and it shows a healthier, more varied and more versatile farm picture than ever before in this state." But 1966 was not a good year for the Louisiana bulletin, or for those of us who read and loved it. Very shortly after its fiftieth-anniversary issue, it was suddenly and a bit mysteriously discontinued.

The February 13, 1974, issue of the *Georgia Farmers and Consumers Bulletin* (established March 1, 1917), celebrated the hundredth anniversary of the Georgia Department of Agriculture with a page of excerpts reprinted from the earliest bulletins. The flowers are much the same as those of the present time—tuberoses, daffodils, clematis, royal purple irises, pink hardy phlox—but since I have been reading the bulletins I have not seen any advertisements for "flue-cured tobacco, old and mellow for chewing and smoking," and you can no longer get, for a dime and a two-cent stamp, enough mixed seed to plant a garden full of cockscomb, four-o'clocks, bachelor's buttons, Jacob's ladder, and prince's feather.

The *Market Bulletin* of the West Virginia Department of Agriculture is published twice a month, but I know nothing of its origins, save that it was entered as second class matter with the postal authorities on February 25, 1918.

The *Florida For Sale, Want, and Exchange Bulletin* "was entered to the mails under permit as an agricultural publication on August 2, 1919, although it was born prior to that time," its feature editor, Debbie Clayton, wrote in answer to my questions. Its name has since been changed to *Market Bulletin*, and it is published semimonthly.

The Connecticut *Market Bulletin*, the only one I know of to be published in the North, was established in 1920. It is not free, and I did not find any advertisements for flowers in the samples sent me in 1960. On the whole, the advertisements in it lack style: "pedigreed Walker foxhound pups"; "winter cabbage plants"; "young pigs from grain-fed stock."

The first issue of the *Agricultural Review* of North Carolina was published in 1925. When I looked it over some twenty years later, I found few flowers in the classified advertisements, and none of any interest. After another ten years or so, at the urging of my friend Hannah Withers, I took another look, finding a wealth of garden flowers and many fascinating native plants from the Blue Ridge Mountains. I have been subscribing to it ever since.

The *Tennessee Market Bulletin* first appeared in 1927. I have not included it with the others, as the classified advertisements are mostly of livestock and farm equipment.

When I wrote to ask about the history of the *Mississippi Market Bulletin*, Charles Shotts sent me a reprint of the first issue, published July 1, 1928. Under the headline, "Here's Your Market Bulletin," Commissioner J. C. Holton wrote:

Starting with this issue, *The Mississippi Market Bulletin* will be a regular visitor in some ten thousand Mississippi farm homes. . . . The Market Bulletin has an important part to play in Mississippi agriculture, and every effort will be made to so operate that it will live up to its obligations. It is primarily planned as a market place for farm products, and will dwell especially on those thousand-and-one things grown on the farm which have no regular and organized channels of market. . . . It is the little things, each of which is small, but which added together will run into millions of dollars, that the Market Bulletin hopes to aid in selling. Chickens, eggs, farm machinery and equipment, surplus cattle and hogs, plants, seeds, preserves and jellies, molasses—the list is almost endless. They are found on every farm, and would be produced in ever-increasing quantities if there were a cash market available. . . . In starting this publication, the State Department of Agriculture is entering no untried field, is undertaking no experiment in philanthropy at the expense of the state. Similar publications are issued from states all around us, and their experience is the surest guide to our own success or failure.

The first issue of the Mississippi bulletin also contained a formal greeting to "the farmers and farm women" of the state from Mr. Holton. It concludes as follows: "The Bulletin is yours. Use it, and encourage your neighbor to do likewise. We hope and feel that it will be of real benefit. . . ."

The December 1, 1969, issue of the bulletin reprints the original first page, together with an account of the bulletin's earliest history and sure success, written by Terry L. Megehee, who begins by calling 1928 "quite a year." In Megehee's account, in 1928,

if a man had $500 in cash, he could buy a new roadster in any color he wanted, just so long as it was black. Calvin Coolidge was President. Newspapers were filled with Rags-to-Riches stories about housewives and sales clerks who were making fortunes on the New York Stock Exchange. An acre of cut-over timberland in Mississippi could be bought for a five-dollar bill, or less, while a pair of good mules would bring $300, or more. Theodore Gilmore Bimbo was Governor. And the first issue of *The Mississippi Market Bulletin* was published.

Its publication, Megehee continued, was received warmly. There were 7,000 charter subscribers, rising to 23,000 within eighteen months. A typical response came three months after the first issue in a letter to Commissioner Holton from a gentleman from Hampton, Mississippi:

FOR THE LORD'S SAKE stop that ad for Sagrain seed we had you put in the Market Bulletin as the folks are wearing out my telephone, using all my time, change and stationery answering inquiries and telling them I have sold out from neighbors within ½ mile and covering the whole state. It is absolutely the most effective medium between farmers that I have ever come in contact with. It won't be long before some politician through the influence of commodity dealers will want its publication suppressed. From an economic standpoint it is one of the most constructive means of exchange between farmers and their commodities that has ever come under my observation.

Mr. Megehee's—or Miss Megehee's?—pleasing article about the enthusiastic response to the bulletin is touched with nostalgia, as he writes of the testimonials of praise from its first subscribers. "Many of the cards and letters bore post marks of hamlets and villages that no longer boast post offices in this, the era of ZIP codes. Sadly, the names of yesterday's crossroad communities read like an obituary of promise: Barto. Cannonsburg. Mashulaville. Auter. Sweatman. Thyatira. Sapa. Perkshire. Big Point. Mileston. . . . " Megehee's litany of places with names now forgotten goes on and on, but it suggests a further point. These early market bulletins speak of times and customs that are long gone, or that are rapidly passing. I have an idea that if someone sat down and read all of the market bulletins since 1928, he would have a rich sense of the social history of the rural Deep South, through the years of the Great Depression to more recent times: the history of people whose names are now recorded only in family Bibles, in the records of county courthouses, on tomb-stones in country cemeteries — and in the yellowed pages of the market bulletins where they sold their mules and their cordwood, their bales of sweet-smelling alfalfa, their old-fashioned daffodils and their yard plants with their poetic country names.

The first issue of the *Alabama Farmers for Sale, Want, and Exchange Bulletin* was published on May 15, 1932. The first page is almost a replica of Mississippi's, with the same letter setting forth the same aims, under the headline "Here is Good News for the Farmers." In the "For Sale" column "large quantities of soy bean hay" are offered; "one dozen peafowl eggs, no special breed" are wanted; and someone wants to barter "50 bushels of velvet beans for a cream separator." When I inquired in 1968, Bruce Jetton, editor of the *Alabama Farmers' Bulletin*, its changed name, wrote me that there were 47,000 subscribers in all fifty states and four foreign countries.

Although it is older than any of the publications I will be treating in the following pages, having been founded in 1900, I will have nothing to say about the Virginia

Department of Agriculture and Commerce *Bulletin*. It is a farmers' monthly magazine consisting of agricultural news, articles, and statistics. There are a few classified advertisements, but with one exception, almost no plants are offered. I mention it here for the sake of the exception, Miss Susie Martin, who rarely fails to advertise in each issue a variety of garden flowers and houseplants. You find them everywhere—people who, like Miss Martin, garden for love.

Elizabeth Lawrence
Charlotte, N.C.
n.d.

The Mississippi Market Bulletin

Sweet Country Names

Years ago Eudora Welty told me about the old ladies who sell flowers through the mail and advertise in the *Mississippi Market Bulletin*, published twice a month by the Mississippi Department of Agriculture. She put my name on the mailing list.

In the market bulletin, farmers advertise their crops, their cattle, their horses and dogs, and their wives list the seeds and bulbs and plants that they sell for pin money. People also list the things they want to buy and the things they are willing to swap. Whole families advertise for work on farms, and homeless people advertise for jobs with room and board. Their advertisements show the customs of the country people, their humor, and their way of speaking. Like Eudora's novels, the market bulletins are a social history of the Deep South. Through them I know the farmers and their dogs, their horses and mules, and the pedigrees of their cattle. I wonder whether the widow with no family ties found a home with an elderly couple needing someone to take care of them; whether the family of cotton pickers found work and a house near school and church; whether the bachelor with no bad habits found a congenial job where the hunting and fishing were good; whether puppies got homes and lost dogs were found. And I wonder who bought the little farm with the pecan trees and good clear well water.

Most of all I like to think about the hard-working farm women who are never too tired, when their farm work is done, to cultivate their flower gardens. They always find time to gather seeds, to dig and pack plants, and to send them off with friendly letters. To all parts of the country they send them off—yard plants, houseplants, and window plants. Reading the flower lists is like reading poetry, for the flowers are called by their sweet country names, many of them belonging to Shakespeare and the Bible.

In *The Golden Apples* Eudora Welty tells about the death and funeral of Miss Katie Rainey, who advertised in the market bulletin. She once wore a pink sunbonnet and sat in a swivel chair by the roadside selling crochet and peaches, muscadines and dewberries, and the little peanuts for boiling. Then the traffic changed. The wrong people took over the road, riding fast in their big trucks, hauling timber to mill. "They were not eaters of muscadines, and did not stop to pass words on the season and what grew."

On the day Miss Katie Rainey died, her daughter Virgie was down on the floor cutting out a dress, and had just announced that she aimed "to get married on my bulb money." Miss Katie felt a sharp stab of pain. She asked Virgie to fan her. Virgie fanned her with the market bulletin.

Dying, Miss Katie went rapidly over the list in it, her list. As though her impatient foot would stamp at each item, she counted it, corrected it, and yet she was about to forget the seasons, and the places things grew. Purple althea cuttings, true box, four colors of cannas for 15¢, moonvine seed by teaspoonful, green and purple jew. Roses: big white rose, little thorn rose, beauty-red sister rose, pink monthly, old-fashioned red summer rose, very fragrant, baby rose. Five colors of verbena, candlestick lilies, milk and wine lilies, blackberry lilies, lemon lilies, angel lilies, apostle lilies. Angel trumpet seed. The red amaryllis.

Faster and faster, Mrs. Rainey thought: Red salvia, four-o'clock, pink Jacob's ladder, sweet geranium cuttings, sword fern and fortune grass, century plants, vase palm, watermelon pink and white crape myrtle, Christmas cactus, golden bell. White Star Jessamine. Snowball. Hyacinthus. Pink fairy lilies. White. The fairy white.

When I read the market bulletins I think about Mrs. Rainey and her flowers, and I think about the wrong people going by on the Mississippi roads and wonder how long the bulletin will continue to come. And when it arrives, twice a month, I turn the pages to see whether Mrs. Radau still has sunbonnet daisies and Voleene Martin still advertises the Texas bell vine. And then, when I find them all there—Mrs. Breland and Mrs. Apperson and Nancy Holder; prince's feather, Jacob's ladder, and four-o'clocks—I feel comforted.

All of those old roses growing in country gardens—I think of Mrs. Rainey whenever I come upon their names in the market bulletins. The sister rose must be the old multiflora called the Seven Sisters because the white buds open into pink flowers and fade to tones of violet, so there are seven colors in a single cluster. There's no telling what will turn up as "the old Burmuda rose" or the "Florida red rose," but "Louis Philippe" is a well-known China rose found in every dooryard. The "old timey bur rose" is the little spreading shrub with small leaves and double rose-colored flowers that is grown in gardens all over the South. My Aunt Letty brought it to us from an old place in Virginia. She called it the chinquapin rose. Now, in some devious way, it has become *Rosa roxburghii*. The old noisette, Maréchal Niel, is sometimes advertised as "the old timey yellow running rose, Marshall Neal." (In the South a running rose is not one that runs; it is one that climbs.) In the market bulletin there are names not to be found in catalogs: the white coronation rose, the lady-of-the-lake, and "the old fashion Betsy rose that blooms all summer." I wish I had room to grow them all.

And all those lilies. In the South almost anything is called a lily; crinums are seldom known by any other name. The candlestick and milk-and-wine lilies are crinums, and so are the angel lilies and the apostle lilies. I suppose candlestick is a corruption of candystick, the common name of *Crinum scabrum*, which has peppermint-striped flowers. Apostle lily, I think, is a name given to almost any crinum with about a dozen flowers to a scape. The milk-and-wine lilies all have milk white flowers with wine-streaked petals. The angel lily is a brightly keeled milk-and-wine with five or six wide open flowers to a scape. I have had it from gardens in North Carolina and from a nursery in Texas. One of the most beautiful of the crinums, it blooms in late summer and fall.

When we lived in Raleigh I made a collection of garden crinums, and I had some correspondence with Mrs. U. B. Evans, who lived on a plantation near Ferriday, Louisiana (Zone 8). She wrote:

I live a long way in the country, about twenty miles from Natchez, and nine miles from the highway and the nearest telephone. On this quiet, cloudy Sunday afternoon, I wish we could sit in front of the fire and talk about the crinums in old gardens. I believe I have seventeen different kinds. They bloom all summer and into the fall. I believe the old-fashioned milk-and-wine lily, with its drooping bells, must have a number of forms. I have one from Natchez that has quite round petals, overlapped, and very broad dark red stripes; the flowers open wide. Another form, found in a yard in Baskin, Louisiana, is the best crinum I have ever seen. It has very wide open pinkish-white blooms, with dark red stripes; as many as fifteen to twenty open at once on stalks from four to five feet tall. By feeding and watering I can bring it into bloom at any time. Several separate bulbs bloomed as many as five times this summer, after it rained. I suppose the one with white petals with narrow red stripes and wide open, star-shaped flowers in late fall is *Crinum fimbriatulum*. We call it the Confederate lily. Another old crinum with deep rose flowers and wide, stiff leaves is supposed to have come from a garden in New Orleans forty years ago. It has narrow, linear petals and stalks six feet and over. Then there is a deep pink crinum that blooms only in October, and when the flowers are cut for the house they last for days.

In spring, before the crinums come into bloom, the Louisiana irises are the show. On a well-drained slope I have a planting six hundred feet long. Violets are another special interest—I have more than fifty different kinds. And I collect old daffodils. I agree with you that exchange with other gardeners is the only way to clarify the information we get from books.

That red amaryllis on Mrs. Rainey's list is often advertised in the market bulletins. It is the old hybrid, *Hippeastrum* × *johnsonii*, called St. Joseph's lily on the Gulf Coast, where it usually blooms by the nineteenth of March, the Feast of St. Joseph. In my garden in Charlotte, it blooms two months later, but it is one of the most permanent and dependable of outdoor bulbs. When the iridescent red flowers are in bloom, I think of Henry Nehrling's account in *My Garden in Florida* of seeing them for the first time, in Houston, Texas, on an April morning in 1879:

> Gardenias bloomed in the gardens and gave off their rich fragrance. The splendor of the tea roses, the bloom of the charming Gloire de Dijon, Maréchal Niel, Chromatella, and other climbing roses on the wide verandas were to me quite overwhelming, since I had just recently quit the raw climate of Chicago. I could scarcely see enough of the great flowered magnolias that decorated the gardens and the romantic shore of Buffalo Bay. The sound of the song of the mocking bird resounded in all the gardens, and cardinals slipped through the thick evergreen foliage of loquat, myrtle, and the Cherokee rose.

Wandering among orange trees and under live oaks dripping Spanish moss, Dr. Nehrling saw in the distance a great patch of glowing red. Quickening his steps, he came upon a large garden in front of a long, low house in the shelter of evergreen trees. Roses and jasmines bloomed over the veranda, and on either side of the path leading to the house were broad beds of beautiful, red trumpet-shaped flowers that glistened in the sunlight as if strewn with gold dust and that gave off an aromatic fragrance. Dr. Nehrling recognized them as Johnson's amaryllis, "an old garden flower in the South, from the Gulf of Mexico to Memphis, Tennessee and Raleigh, North Carolina."

Eudora got a blue wonder lily from the market bulletin. She said it had never bloomed and she was still wondering. We consulted Ruth Dormon, Caroline Dormon's sister-in-law, who said it must be the seven-year hyacinth (*Scilla hyacinthoides*) found in old gardens in the Deep South and said to bloom but once in seven years. Later another friend, who also had it from Mississippi, sent me a slide showing a scape of small blue-violet flowers, close together in the bud, but the wide open lower ones well separated and on pedicels more than an inch long. The scapes bear from fifty to a hundred and fifty flowers.

Scilla hyacinthoides, from the Mediterranean region, has been in cultivation in England since 1585. At one time it was grown by California nurserymen. Cecil Houdyshel listed it for the first time in his little bulb catalog in 1941. "We were long doubtful of this rare species," he said. "It is one of the finest bulbs for the outside garden as it is perfectly hardy in the North. It is a strong grower, and will even recover when left out of the ground for a year.

Take my advice and plant it." I took his advice, but it never bloomed. One of my bulletin correspondents, Elsie Hassam writes that it did bloom in her garden in Alabama, but she wintered it in a tub. I have since read that it needs a thorough baking in summer, or else the bulbs must be taken up in the fall and dried for a few days in the sun.

Fairy lilies—(the pink, the white, and also the yellow—) are the rain lilies, the little zephyranthes that spring up after showers. B. Y. Morrison said they should always be grown in quantity, as they grow in the hills of Mexico, in meadows in parts of the South, or in his own garden at Pass Christian. "The lawns have been mowed," he wrote early one June, "and the late azaleas are in bloom with sheets of *Habranthus tubispathus* and all the zephyranthes in sheets of pink. We have one zephyranthus that sows itself freely in patches of solid color. It came from the USDA years ago, without a name." In my own garden there is room for only a few of each kind, but I like to have them surprise me with their small and sudden flowers; they make no demands, and take up so little space. When I find one of the delicately colored flowers in bloom, I pick it, put it in a little glass bottle, and take it from room to room in order not to lose a moment of its brief and fragile existence.

The blackberry lily (*Belamcanda chinensis*) is hardy, belongs to country gardens everywhere, and has even escaped to the woods. Its ephemeral leopard-spotted flowers are followed by shiny black fruits that look so much like the real thing that I am sure they must fool even the birds.

The old ladies who advertise the surprise lily as "pink

amaryllis Hallie" must have had it for a long time, for it has been years since *Lycoris squamigera* was called *Amaryllis hallii*. As Hallie is a popular girl's name in the South, I expect they think it was named for some Miss Hallie instead of Dr. Hall. The red spider lily is *Lycoris radiata*. Through an old mistake, a few country gardeners still advertise it as the Guernsey lily (*Nerine sarniensis*). I think the bulb they call the white magic lily is the white lycoris, and the white spider lily is the native hymenocallis—a confused genus, with both spring-blooming and fall-blooming species, of which I grow several sorts. One of my letter-writing friends, Mrs. J. Norman Henry, has collected bulbs from Indiana as well as all the states of the South, and she has grown them successfully in her garden in Gladwyn, Pennsylvania, for more than twenty years. "I am glad to say that all my hymenocallis bloom lustily," she wrote me. "Dr. Hamilton Traub says a number of them are new species. He has named one of them *Hymenocallis henryae* after me. I am sending you a bulb. I found it a good many years ago in western Florida, growing with about four inches of sandy peat soil on top of it."

Among the so-called lilies in the country gardens of the Lower South are two members of the ginger family. One, the butterfly lily (*Hedychium coronarium*), is hardy in North Carolina. All it needs to make it bloom from August to frost is a fair amount of sun and plenty of water. It also needs plenty of room, for it grows to a height of five feet. It also spreads, but never gets a chance to become truly invasive, since someone is always begging a root. In spite of its size, Andrebe Grabe says in the *Complete Book of House Plants* that she has brought it to bloom in a south window in November, by planting it outside in summer and repotting it late in August when the buds began to form. "The white orchidlike flowers were unbelievably fragrant," she writes, "perfuming the entire house with a delicate, spicy scent. They bloomed in a crown of five or six at a time. After the blooming I was about to cut off the stalk when I noticed another full crown coming from the same stalk." They need full sun, she says, average potting soil, routine fertilizing, and frequent and copious drenching.

Hedychiums are also called ginger lilies, as are the curcumas. What the market bulletins call hidden lily is *Curcuma petiolata*, whose fragrant, little yellow flowers are hidden by violet bracts. It is as hardy (they say) as the butterfly lily, and a more convenient size for pots.

Sometimes the supposedly tender plants of southern gardens can be grown in protected places in the North. One of these is the pineapple lily (*Eucomis comosa*), which has proved hardy in the Harvard Botanic Gardens, where it blooms in August, just as it does in North Carolina. In a shady border the clumps of wide leaves are ornamental, and the tufted columns of fragrant greenish white flowers are attractive for a month or more.

The purple-flowered gladiolus species that the farm women sell as Jacob's ladder must have come from England, bringing its name with it, for English cottagers have grown it by that name since the beginning of the seventeenth century. Here in North Carolina, it blooms in early May, in the interval between spring and summer, when its brilliant red-violet flowers, almost a true purple, are very welcome. I always thought it to be tender, since it comes from the Mediterranean region, but I have recently read a report that it is hardy in the North and need not be dug up and stored in the fall. Its botanical name is *Gladiolus byzantinus.*

Mrs. Rainey's angel trumpet is one of the shrubby daturas. The Spanish settlers called the great drooping bells floripondio, heavy flower. They said it is the moon's lover, because it blooms by night and the flowers are most fragrant when the moon is full. *Brugmansia suaveolens*, the common species in gardens and courtyards along the Gulf and in southern California, is a treelike shrub growing to fifteen feet or more, but usually less. *Brugmansia sanguinea*, a smaller plant with flame-colored flowers, is a choice greenhouse plant. It is one of the real rarities that the farm women sometimes offer.

The century plant (*Agave americana*), of course, does not really take a century to bloom, but it takes its own time, usually about fifteen years, although one of the women who advertised it in the market bulletin wrote me that hers "bloomed after twenty-six years, the flower stalk as thick as a sapling and growing to twenty-eight feet." The flower scape springs from the center of a huge clump of blue-green, spine-tipped leaves, a clump that grows broader every year and sometimes reaches a diameter of twelve feet or more before it flowers and then dies.

Mrs. Rainey's "fortune grass" must be fountain grass, *Pennisetum setaccum*. Her "sword fern" would be Boston fern, *Nephrolepis exaltata bostoniensis*, which grows everywhere in Mississippi, indoors and out, and appears frequently in the market bulletin. Other ferns are often listed. I'm not sure what many of them are, except that the Japanese climbing fern is *Lygodium japonicum*, one of the most beautiful plants in southern gardens, except that in the Lower South it spreads itself so freely as to become troublesome. In my own garden, newly set plants seldom survive a single winter, but an established plant, a gift from a friend in Oxford, Mississippi, has gone through twelve winters, one of them with temperatures near zero. When the foliage turns brown, usually around Christmas, I cut the stems to the ground. Then in spring, between February and April, depending on the weather, new stems come up and climb to twelve feet or more, interlacing as they go. The fertile leaflets are so much more finely divided than the sterile ones that the effect is one of two different plants growing together. The house plant in the trade as *Lygodium scandens* is, I think, *L. japonicum*. If I grew things indoors, this would be my first choice. In the garden it grows even in deep shade, and in the house it will tolerate a north window. Still speaking of ferns, the holly fern (*Cyrtomium falcatum*) that I got through the market bulletin grows finer every year, but the leather fern (*Rumohra adiantiformis*) barely holds its own. Perhaps it should be given further trial. Perhaps not.

*

That subscription Eudora Welty gave me to the market bulletin testified to the hold it had over the imagination of her Mrs. Rainey. It also seized my own imagination, as I became familiar with the way the farm women who advertised in its poorly printed pages of cheap newsprint classified the plants they grew, not according to the ways of botanists, but according to their uses. There are, for example, yard plants. There are box plants. And there are window plants.

None of these classifications is much of a surprise. Yard plants are simply plants that grow out of doors: yard moss, yard ferns, yard fuchsias, yard ivy, and yard asparagus, which is advertised as perennial and hardy. Window plants grow indoors. One collection offers "window vines, unknown fern, and a sermon-on-the-mount." Box plants are grown on the porch in boxes. A "blue box plant" might be most anything—probably some trailing plant with blue flowers, such as *Vinca major*.

"My husband is an invalid," Mrs. Ida Dawkins wrote in the "Flowers Wanted" column in one issue. "He has been in bed for six years. I like box flowers. Would be glad if someone would send me a few cuttings. I lost most of mine last winter."

Mrs. Dawkins' appeal reminded me of Miss Gertrude Jekyll's story, in *Wood and Garden*, of the factory lad who advertised in a mechanical paper that he wanted a tiny garden, "as full of interest as might be," in a window box; that he knew nothing about growing plants, and would be grateful for advice as to what to grow in a box three feet long and ten inches wide. Miss Jekyll found his longing to have some growing things in his tenement window irresistible. She evidently thought that a rock garden would offer the greatest interest in the smallest space, for she sent him some mossy and some silvery saxifrages, a few small bulbs, and some stones. In the box he was instructed to construct two hills (one slightly higher than the other) with rocky tops and a "longish valley with a sunny and a shady side."

I cannot conceive of a more delightful scheme, or of one less likely to succeed. When I find the practical Miss Jekyll recommending small saxifrages, the most difficult of rock plants, for growing in the sooty air of a great manufacturing town in the north of England, it convinces me that even the gods can nod. I would like to know how long they survived. It seems to me that the factory lad would have fared better with some indestructible sedums in place of the saxifrages, even though they might not be so interesting, but it is easier to see the lack of wisdom in someone else's choice than to make a sensible one yourself.

When I began to look about my garden for something for Mrs. Dawkins, something that would live over the winter, be attractive all of the growing season, and not take up much space, I found few plants that filled all of the requirements. I finally settled upon a clump of the hardy begonia (*Begonia grandis*), a clump of *Oxalis tetraphylla*, some forget-me-nots, and a cutting of the beautiful little ivy called Needlepoint. If she watered them well and picked off all the dead flowers, the forget-me-nots would bloom until frost. The begonia wouldn't bloom until August, but its foliage is stunning. The oxalis has charming pink flowers and purple-banded leaflets over a long period, and the ivy would give her something to enjoy over the winter.

*

"Spice-smelling geraniums" of all kinds are offered in the market bulletin, as is the strawberry-geranium (or begonia), which is not a geranium (nor a begonia). It is *Saxifraga stolonifera*, mother-of-thousands or roving sailor, which is hardy with me and very useful in dark, neglected parts of the garden. Another begonia that is not a begonia is *Justicia carnea*, the plume plant, which Viva Mae Pipkins offers as the pine-bur begonia. "It blooms from the last of May through early winter," she says, "and has rose-colored flowers shaped like pine burrs." It is root hardy in Mississippi and even in Charlotte, though it is slow to recover in these parts. In the North, Ernesta Drinker Ballard says (in *Garden in Your House*), it is "decorative, but scarcely justifies the considerable space it takes on a sunny windowsill, since it blooms only in summer."

Other begonias, real ones, that the farm women offer are the lettuce-leaf, the elm-leaf, and the grape-leaf; rex or painted-leaf; Catalina, Medora, and Lucerna. One woman offers a collection of "six small plants, some in bloom. One Indian Bride, very rare, white flowers, bronze foliage. One double rose. One double red, green foliage. One rose flowering, bronze foliage. One red flowering, bronze foliage. One pink, green glossy foliage, makes a good bedding plant." Then there are cacti of all kinds: the bow cactus, the crowfoot cactus, the rattail, cattail, foxtail, and squirreltail cactus; the snake, the peanut, the dribble, the fan, and the star cactus. And there is one for every season: the February, Easter, May Day, Mother's Day, Thanksgiving, and Christmas cactus. And more: the Chinese temple, the cob ball, the chimney cactus; the pencil, the grape, and the little rice cactus. Some, like the crown-of-thorns cactus, are not cacti at all but belong to other families. *Pedilanthus tithymaloides*, sometimes called redbird cactus, usually appears in the bulletins as devil's-backbone or devil's-bone.

The favorite market bulletin window ferns are the sword, lace, leather, asparagus, curley, and fluffy-ruffles ferns—and the baby-breath fern, whatever that is. Occasionally I come upon some rare species such as the Bermuda maidenhair fern (*Adiantum bellum*), a miniature that grows to about six inches, needs shade and lime, and likes water in winter and rest in summer. *Hortus Third* says

A. bellum is generally *A. raddianum* 'Pacottii'.

Window plants usually go by their common names, such as mother-in-law plant (*Dieffenbachia*), chicken gizzard (*Iresine herbstii*), shrimp plant (once *Beloperone guttata*, now *Justicia brandegeana*), chenille plant (*Acalypha hispida*), pussy ears (*Cyanotis somaliensis*), and aluminum plant (*Pilea cadierei*), but some names, such as airplane plant, seem to be local to Mississippi. *Achimenes* is commonly known as widow's-tears, but in the market bulletin it appears as monkey-face plant or monkey-face petunia. In Louisiana they call it bleeding petunia.

I think the house plant with the most names must be *Rhoeo spathacea* (formerly *Rhoeo discolor*), which is called man-in-boat, three-men-in-a-boat, Moses-in-a-cradle, Moses-on-a-raft, Moses-in-the-bullrushes, and Christ-in-a-hamper. One advertiser called it moose-in-boat.

*

In Eudora Welty's *Losing Battles*, the house plants among Granny's birthday presents all came out of the market bulletin. She complained about getting the same old Christmas cactus she was so sick and tired of. She also got a speckled geranium, an improved Boston fern packed in a bread wrapper, a prayer plant, a double touch-me-not, and a tub of recently dug hyacinth bulbs. The hyacinths would be the china blue kind that grow in old gardens. On Granny's porch, market bulletin morning glories climbed, and ferns in hanging baskets were strung across the front. Lace-leaf verbenas overflowed the concrete pipes at the foot of the steps, rows of cannas bloomed around the house, and red salvias, lemon lilies, and prince's feathers were tightly planted in the flower beds. Down by the pasture, hummingbirds hovered over the orange montbretias without seeming to touch a flower.

Gloria Renfro, the wife of Granny's oldest great-grandson, had been rescued by Miss Julia Mortimer, the teacher at Banner School who boarded her and sent her to high school. Miss Julia had fruit bushes and flower plants and good seed for sale through the market bulletin, sending out letters and packages all over Mississippi. Gloria was expected to do her part. She hoed and dug and took cuttings, wrapping the newly dug plants in fresh violet leaves and bread paper and packing them moist in soda boxes and matchboxes. She saved the seed and measured it in an old spoon.

Whenever I read the market bulletins, I think of Gloria and Miss Julia Mortimer. I see the ladies who sell flowers through the mail in the setting of Granny's old house with galleries that run its full width, back and front, and the morning glories on the porch, and the big China trees at the gate posts.

*

The farm women are great letter writers, and usually answer (delightfully and often at length) if a stamped and addressed envelope is enclosed. One advertiser says, "If information is wanted, enclose ten cents," which seems fair enough, but usually questions are answered freely, willingly, and with love. I think my only unanswered letter is one that was returned from a crossroads post office. I expect the lady had died, for I had gotten her name out of an old issue. I can never bear to throw away old market bulletins, and I am always going back to them.

I thought Mrs. Ottice Breland's sweet horsemen must be horsemint, so I wrote to ask if I had guessed right and to beg for some more local names for a book I meant to write. She replied:

> Concerning your Flower Book I am a true flower lover and grower, and I am glad to help you in any way I can, but I might send you a bunch of names, and you would already have them. Let me know about your book, when you finish, how many names are in it. The flower you sent me is sweet horsemint. There are other kinds of mints, but this is the only one I have. I will send you bride bouquet, the calico border plant, and weeping Mary. Weeping Mary is advertised by some as purple butterfly (buddleia).

Bride bouquet proved to be bouncing bet (*Saponaria officinalis*), a wayside flower with many old names — goodbye-summer, wild sweet william, and lady-at-the-gate. In Georgia it is called sally-at-the-gate, but I never heard bride bouquet before. Mrs. Breland grows the handsome double form that was cultivated in English gardens in the seventeenth century. On summer evenings the fragrance of the flowers is so intense that they were described by one old writer as "fulsomely sweet."

The calico border plant is the common yarrow, *Achillea millefolium*. The genus was named for Achilles, who used the leaves to treat his soldiers' wounds. Yarrow has been put to many other uses, including brewing beer and making a tea to cure colds and rheumatism. People have chewed the leaves to relieve toothaches and to drive away sad thoughts. Another old name for it is nosebleed, for plant lore has it that the leaves, if held to the nose, will make it bleed and thus relieve migraine. I wonder if the pink form of this yarrow is what some country women list as pink Queen Anne's lace.

When I asked Mrs. Breland about the Virginia rose, which she describes as making a small tree with large, double pink blooms in fall, she offered to send me a plant.

> I am still in the mud with sick folks, so I am late again answering your letter. I am going to send you sometime next week, I hope, a moon lily and a Virginia rose. I would say put the Virginia rose in a large pot or bucket, and keep it in shade until it begins to grow. When it starts to grow it likes sun. Keep it in the house this winter, and put it out next spring. It will bloom next fall, and will come up from the roots each spring if protected from freezes. I paid a dollar for one plant that is supposed to bloom this fall, but I don't think it will. A neighbor sent me some moon lily seeds real late, so the plant I am sending you is small. Cover the moon lily good with green bushes until it starts to grow. It will come up from the roots each spring. In winter, cover the roots with leaf mold, straw, old sacks, or anything. It may bloom late. Guess you are tired of my advice on growing plants, but if I can help you don't fail to let me know. I will be at your service.

She signed herself "a true flower lover," and added a postscript: "I am going to see my sister tomorrow. Maybe I can gather your plants and get them off Wednesday or Thursday."

Mrs. Breland must have gotten them off on Wednesday, for they arrived on Saturday, carefully labeled and damp-packed. The moon lily, as I guessed, was *Datura inoxia* subsp. *inoxia*, still generally sold under its old name *D. meteloides*, a perennial native to the Southwest from Texas to California. It is easily grown from seed, and with me will bloom the first season. In the North, it can be grown as an annual if the seeds are sown indoors, but in cool northern summers the plants may not bloom. The moon lily is low and spreading, with wide, gray leaves and lavender-tinted stems, and blossoms like great white trumpets faintly washed in lavender. The flowers open at dusk and pour their fragrance all over the garden. But the moon lily should never be grown in a garden where there are childen, for it is as poisonous as it is beautiful.

The Virginia rose proved to be the Confederate rose, *Hibiscus mutabilis*—called *mutabilis* because the flowers open white, turn pink, and then red by evening. I shall take Mrs. Breland's advice about keeping it indoors the first winter, for it comes from the tropics, but after that I mean to leave it to its fate. In ordering plants from the market bulletin, incidentally, it must be remembered that there are three zones of plant hardiness in Mississippi: Zone 9 along the Gulf Coast, Zone 8 in the center of the state, and Zone 7 in the northern part. Mrs. Breland lives in Neely, which is Zone 8. Charlotte is in the same zone, but she is in the southern half, we in the northern, and this difference sometimes is crucial for borderline plants such as *Hibiscus mutabilis*.

Mrs. Breland is the kind of gardener who grows some of everything, but especially daylilies and camellias, which she collects. Once she advertised "Chinese pink morning glory seeds, large green leaves eight inches across, vine soft thorny kind, very pretty and makes a quick shade." I sent for some, and when they came there was a letter in the envelope: "Soak the seed overnight before planting, and put a cloth over the hill to keep the dirt soft and deep. Put water on the cloth every day until they begin coming up. The first leaves are so large they don't come up through dry hard dirt very good. If you haven't seen this vine you are in for a surprise."

Mrs. Breland also sent a plant she called Turk's-cap, which I already knew from Miss Nancy Holder, who had advertised it as "bright red ladies' eardrops." When I asked Miss Holder to send me a flower, she wrote: "Kind Flower Lover, I am sending you a twig of Ladies' eardrops with a tiny flower on it. The flowers are about an inch and a half in summer days, but this one is late on the bush, and small. Thanks for writing me." I ordered plants, and when they came wrote to tell Miss Holder how fresh they were. "I am glad your order was in good shape," she replied. "I pack in deep moss, and it requires more postage but the plants go through much better. . . . Thanks for writing me, and I trust you get a good grow."

Later, I sent a specimen of this plant to Dr. Sigmond Solymosy at the University of Southwestern Louisiana. He identified it as *Malvaviscus arboreus drummondii*, a shrub native to Texas and Mexico. It is called Mexican apple because the edible fruits look like tiny red apples. Another species, M. *arboreus mexicanus*, is showier but less hardy. (*Hortus Third* says Turk's-cap is M. *pendulifloras*.) In *Flower and Vegetable Garden*, James Vick describes M. *arboreus drummondii* as a bedding plant and "a good house plant that blooms continuously. The flower is bright scarlet, and remains in perfect condition for a long time. In pot culture it usually grows about two feet high, but when placed in the garden it grows quite strong."

Lady's-eardrop is of course also an old name for another plant, the fuchsia. In *Flowers and Flower Lore*, a book where

I find many of the old names that turn up in the market bulletins (sometimes attached to the same plants, sometimes to different ones), Hilderic Friend reminisces about the fuchsias that went under this name in his childhood:

> Who has not heard the old folk speak of the Fuchsia as the Lady's Eardrop? I distinctly remember when I was a lad going from time to time with my mother on a visit to my grandmother, an elderly lady, and one who was very proud of her flower-garden. She almost always took us to see her Lady's Eardrop, as she preferred to call her Fuchsia, when it was in bloom. The older people in Devonshire still speak of the plant under the same name, and I was told on the borders of Dartmore quite recently that it is not many years since Lady's Eardrop was the only name there known. In American works on botany, too, the Fuchsia is often thus spoken of, the people who emigrated from England years ago probably carrying the familiar name with them.

Friend is right, for Alphonso Wood in 1876 called the fuchsia lady's-eardrop in his *Flora Atlantica*. And I can easily see how this old name was transferred from the fuchsia to the drooping red flowers of *Malvaviscus arboreus drummondii*.

Another plant I got from Mrs. Breland, many years ago when I was living in Raleigh, was the Jerusalem thorn (*Parkinsonia aculeata*), a little, prickly tree with fine, twice-pinnate leaves and long drooping racemes of fragrant golden flowers. It did not survive its first winter, but it is much planted in the Low Country and has even escaped into the wild from gardens in Beaufort County, South

Carolina. Why the genus should have been named for a sixteenth-century herbalist who died more than a hundred years before it was brought to England from tropical America, I cannot imagine, and Jerusalem thorn seems equally inappropriate.

After some time went by when I didn't see any of Mrs. Breland's advertisements in the market bulletin, I wrote to ask if she could send me a tuber of her potato vine, described in an old issue as having "green heart-shaped leaves up to eight inchs long; seed balls grow on vine."

Her son answered my letter. He said his mother had had a stroke and now lived with him. He sent me two round, silvery tubers, the size of a very small new Irish potato. "I hope this is what you want," he wrote. "She says the price is about fifty cents."

The vine was the air potato, *Dioscorea bulbifera*, native to tropical Africa. I had tried it once, years ago, but it is not hardy in these parts. In Florida it makes a quick screen and a dense shade.

*

Mrs. Grady Stamps, of Bogue Chitto, advertised the moon lily as night glow. When I ordered some seed, she wrote:

> It is like angel trumpet but stays low and spreading. The large white funnel-shaped blooms open in summer in late afternoon, when it gets cooler, and perfume the air. My mother used to have them, we called them moon-flower. When I saw night-glow advertised in the Louisiana bulletin I ordered some seed and found it was the same thing. I got some seed of climbing hibiscus from another lady in Louisiana, and it was the same plant I saw in bloom

in Houston, Texas, when I lived over there during the last war. It grows up in long switches; has to be by a fence or something to hold it up, or stake and tie. Has large single blooms in a wine or maroon color, right pretty. Cold kills it down. I haven't had it to come back from roots like the other hibiscus. I'll put in a few seed.

I planted the seeds of the climbing hibiscus in April, and one of the several plants that came up grew to a long switch more than six feet tall, but the early November frost killed the whole stalk just as the buds were ready to burst. I sent one of the pretty, five-fingered leaves to Caroline Dorman, who said it was called sky-high and that it grew in a garden of one of her friends, in Saline. Late the next September, she wrote:

> May Nichol's sky-highs are in bloom right now. They are five inches across, a strange color, almost magenta, but with a maroon center and veining, the whole effect rather stunning. The broad petals overlap and are slightly ruffled. The stalks are about eight feet tall, and fall over if not staked. Now, what they are, and where they came from, is another of the mysteries of things found in old country gardens.

Dr. Solymosy solved the mystery for us. "I have identified your 'climbing hibiscus' as *Hibiscus radiatus* cv. 'flore pleno'," he wrote. "Its origin cannot be traced, but it was first found in Jamaica, growing in cultivation, and probably came to our area through the Creoles, who in the old days had plantations in Haiti and other places."

Mrs. Stamps said she would be glad to have seed of anything I have that is new—meaning new to her—so I looked around the garden to see what was going to seed and found fennel and *Clematis texensis*. Mrs. Stamps wrote me right back:

> I never did have the fennel, and the clematis seed you sent are larger than any I have seen. Must be something new and different. I do hope I get some up. I love to work with flowers, advertise, and get letters from people. Some people write letters when ordering, some send free seed along. I give good measure and free seed, too. I turn my flower money back into more flowers. I have a friend in Texas that swaps plants with me, and a pen pal in Indiana that sends me peonies and lilies. As long as I can, I'll work with my flowers, but I am about to get disabled to work much in them like I used to, so I want bulbs and perennials that will stay there. I must stop now, or I won't have room to enclose some seed. I love to give as well as receive.

A little box of mixed seed was enclosed. I recognized the thin pods of torenia and the round black seed of the balloon vine, which has a white heart printed on it, but I didn't recognize the curious little, beaked fruit of the clock vine (*Thunbergia alata*), though I must have seen it in my garden. Mrs. Stamps calls it black-eyed susan, and the torenia she calls wishbone flower. She knows the name torenia, she said: "I just couldn't think of that name when I wrote the ad. And when I describe anything, they leave it all out and just put the name and price. Such ads as dogs, they put in the whole long description."

Mrs. Stamps sent me seeds of the marble vine, but they didn't come up, perhaps because it is a half-hardy

annual and I put them in the ground too early. Caroline
Dorman said it did not do much for her either, but that it
was lovely in the garden of her friend May Nichols. "May
is just two and a half miles from me," she said, "but her
soil is entirely different—that wonderful coarse, brown-
ish sand that wild flowers love. I'm sure it is neutral or
only slightly acid, for dogwoods don't like it." The marble vine is a member of the gourd family, and its little
round, green-and-white striped fruits, which hang on
the lacy vines from midsummer until frost, look much
like oversized gooseberries. The botanical name is *Diplocyclos palmatus.*

I asked Mrs. Stamps about the plant she calls devil's-
pincushion, and she replied:

> I am sending you leaves and the bloom burr. I hope
> you can tell what the flower looks like. It is an annual
> that comes from seed every year. The seeds fall off
> and new plants come up. It used to grow in a
> fenced-in lot around a tenant's house on my Dad's
> place. We did not know what it was called. If they
> had a name for it I don't remember. I was a kid then.
> We lost seed of it and did not see it any more. My
> brother took over the place after my Dad died, and
> several years after that his wife gave me some seed of
> what she called devil's pincushion. It may have
> another name but it is the same plant we had before.
> There will be three to five sticky balls on one stalk.
> When they are dried, I break them down below the
> burrs to make winter bouquets. They can be silvered,
> or dipped in paint. I hope I have described them so
> you can understand. I guess it has the right name,
> because the burrs will stick to your hand like the

devil when you try to get the seed out. You can throw the seeds out in the garden, over the beds or in rows, and they come up. They are all down in the woods and volunteer in the garden. Some grow taller than I am.

The handsome stalk that Mrs. Stamps sent me was perfectly fresh, so I sent it on to—once again—Dr. Solymosy, who identified it as *Leonotis nepetifolia*, a native of tropical Africa which has been naturalized in the South from Tennessee and North Carolina to Florida and Louisiana. When I gave her this information, Mrs. Stamps wrote:

> I guess that long name of the devil's pincushion must be the botanical name. They always have another name than the one we go by. I never know what kind of a plant they are when they put the big names on them in the bulletin. In catalogs some give both. Wish I knew how to get those botanical names to all flowers. If I have anything else odd you might use I'll let you know. I am glad to help you.

Later, I found an advertisement for "two large stone pots of devil's pincushion, blooming size. Winter does not kill."

"I imagine that devil's pincushion that lady advertised is a cactus," Mrs. Stamps wrote. "This one I have is not hardy."

I asked Mrs. Stamps if her feather vine was the silver-lace vine (*Polygonum aubertii*). She replied:

> No, it is not the silver-lace vine. I have that too. I ordered one once. It makes seed and takes over the place. I am sending seeds and leaves of the feather

vine, but the bloom is over. Let them dry, and see if they feather out like they do on the vine here. The vine has white blooms and grows wild all over the country here, all along the road in some places.

The feather vine, her description made clear, was one of several possible wild or naturalized clematises.

When I asked Mrs. Stamps whether she had advertised in the bulletins before the Second World War, she said no, that she was in Texas then.

My husband worked in the shipyard and we saved our money. We came home in 1945 and bought ten acres of land. We had the timber sawed off for lumber to help out on our house. Got it so we could move in. Had more done all along. Then I started to grow flowers—had lots of petunias come up volunteer. I advertised in a county paper, and people came out and bought them and other things I had enough of. Then I heard of the Mississippi and Louisiana bulletins one could get free. I sent for them, and about 1949 I advertised some seeds. I have been at it ever since. I sell my seed most of the time ten cents a package or three packages for twenty-five cents. I have passion vine, (we used to call it May pop), sky high, tall yellow daisies, four o'clocks, pink penstemon, priscilla or red curly coleus, Virginia rose, red yard fuchsia, night jessamine, bittersweet vine, cashmere bouquet, and others. I have lots of wild flowers, some I don't know the name of. It's been so dry all summer, I won't have many different kinds of seeds to sell this fall. Some did not come up; some came up and died; some came up and could not grow.

The small showers we sometimes have don't go deep. It thundered this evening, but only a few drops fell. We did not get to plant much for the fall garden, and did not make much from the spring garden to can and freeze. I will close now. . . . Your friend, Lucy Stamps.

"I guess you think I don't want to answer your letter," Mrs. Stamps wrote when I asked about her trumpet vine. "Every day I say I have got to write to you, and then put it off again. We have two kinds of trumpet vine. They grow wild—one long straight leaf has orange colored trumpet blossoms, and a scalloped leaf same color blooms." The straight leaf is *Bignonia capreolata*, the cross vine. A cross section of the stem shows a structure in the center in the form of a Maltese cross. The leaves hold on all winter, but turn a dark wine color in cold weather. The flowers appear in April, in profusion when the vine grows on a wall, but less freely, and usually out of sight, when it climbs into tall trees. The scalloped leaf is *Campsis radicans*, the trumpet vine. It is also called cow-itch, and Mrs. Lounsberry says, in *Southern Wild Flowers and Trees*, that country people believe it poisons the milk of cows that eat the foliage. I find no evidence for this belief, but Muenscher says, in *Poisonous Plants of the United States*, that cases of dermatitis have been reported from handling the leaves and flowers. In any case, both the cross vine and the trumpet vine have value, as long as they can be kept in hand, because they are self-climbing, sticking to wood or masonry without support. Both are brilliant in bloom, and both are ruinous once they are left to themselves.

In answer to my question about medicinal plants, Mrs. Stamps wrote:

No, I don't use herbs in tea or any way, or for medicine. I have a few mullein plants. A lady from Jackson ordered mullein leaves from me about two years ago. I wish I had asked her what she used them for—oh yes, would you call sassafras an herb? I get roots from it in early spring and make tea. Anything I can help you with, let me know. I'll try not to wait so long next time—been canning. Your friend, Mrs. Lucy Stamps.

I did not hear from Mrs. Stamps for some time, until, in January, 1975, she wrote again, after I inquired about her.

I am by myself now. I lost my husband the sixteenth of December. He was carried to the hospital the morning before Thanksgiving, and never got to come home. We would have been married fifty years next March. I have just not had a chance to answer. So many coming and going, and too bad most of the time to go out to the mail box in the mornings. We have had so much rain, and we are having many hard freezes. The sun has been shining today but the clouds are going over it now. I was sick two years, never worked in flowers much, so I forgot lots of names. . . . I don't know much about botanical names. I just love flowers and wherever I go if I find anything different I beg or swap. That's how I got started selling seeds and plants through the market bulletin. First I ordered from different people. They were so prompt. Always a nice thank-you note with the order. The seeds and plants always in good shape.

When I had more plants than I needed I thought it would be interesting to sell. And it is! It makes mail time more fun and gives me a little extra change.

*

When Eudora Welty put my name on the market bulletin mailing list, she put her agent Diarmuid Russell's name on too. He called our attention to the advertisements for old-fashioned California beer seed. "Do not let these people out of your sight," he wrote. "I can see the plant clearly. It grows to about four feet. It hasn't, as you might think, got fleshy leaves, but rather delicate frondy affairs that spring out of the stiff, brittle stalk, rather like bamboo. The flowers come only once in every three years, and in those years the beer is bock."

I once wrote to one of the advertisers to ask what beer seed is. She said it is a seed about the size of popcorn that has been popped. You put it in a fruit jar full of sweetened water, and it is enough to serve four or five. If you drink too much, she said, it will make you drunk. I sent her a quarter, but the seeds were not at all like popcorn. They were sticky and granular and of a pale amber color. I sent them on to Mr. Russell, who wrote that he had planted them in his garden. He added that if I would send him a whiskey plant, he wouldn't trouble me further.

Later I began to wonder what beer seed really was. None of my friends in the Deep South could tell me. "Don't know," Caroline Dorman wrote. "I always thought it was a thing like yeast that just 'multiplied'—not the seed of a plant." She proved to be right, but I still wanted to know what the "thing" that multiplied *was*, and where it comes from. So I wrote to another advertiser, Miss

Bergie Barlowe, and asked whether beer seed comes from a plant, and, if so, whether she had any plants for sale. A letter signed T. C. Barlowe came by return mail, with a free sample enclosed. "Dear Madam," Mr. Barlowe wrote, "Bergie has gone to Jackson today, so I will answer your letter. Beer seed makes drinks, not flowers. You can place these in a glass jar, fill with water and about a tablespoon of sugar and the same of syrup. Let it stand two or three days, then it is ready to drink."

Grateful, but still unenlightened, I wrote to Miss Mary Meadows. I told her that I was not in the market for beer seed, but wanted to know what it comes from. "If you make it, what do you make it out of?" I asked. She replied with a sample and a recipe. "It is a seed that makes a soft drink. It goes up and down in the syrup mixture and works only in HOMEMADE SYRUP. Sugar kills the seed. Seed makes good pies. If handled right will grow gallons of seed."

I then wrote to Miss Zettie May Sanders, who answered, "So pleased to answer your inquiry. The beer seed comes from a plant, the sugar cane. It is from the dripping of the boiling sugar when found in the bottom of the sugar cane. I have been told this by an eighty-year-old man. It is all I can tell you."

So Mr. Russell is right. The plant is rather like bamboo. But it is one offering in the market bulletins that still remains quite mysterious to me.

*

I ordered mountain daisies from Mrs. Netherland, and when they came I couldn't tell what they were. They grow very tall, she says, and multiply and reseed. "They are used for background planting, and bloom in the fall when nothing much is in bloom. Each branch of large yellow daisies will make a bouquet. They are so bright and cheerful that people often want to take pictures." I hope I will be able to find out what they are.

My friends in the Far South always think Charlotte is in the Far North, though it is in Zone 8, the same as theirs. "All these plants are hardy," Mrs. Netherland (who lives in Roxie, Mississippi, near Natchez) wrote, "but in your part of the country they may need some winter protection. Set them out as soon as you receive them. Do not let the roots dry out. Put some dead leaves or old hay around the roots and let just the tops stick out. I wish you luck with your plants." I told Mrs. Netherland that the plants came in perfect condition and asked her to describe the alum tree she listed. She replied:

> Thank you for your kind letter. I've never mailed a package that far a distance. I worried for fear they wouldn't reach you in good shape. The alum tree is a tree grown for shade, a rapid grower that was given to me years ago by a friend. Some people call it a candletree. When it blooms the long spikes of yellowish flowers stand up all over the tree like candles. I have noticed that bees are very much attracted to them. In the fall the leaves turn all gorgeous colors— red, orange, and even purple, and the black husks burst and fall away from the round white seeds. I am sending you some seeds, and when the time comes I will try to send flowers and leaves.

The seeds proved to be those of the Chinese tallow tree (*Sapium sebiferum*), sometimes called the candleberry tree, because the Chinese make candles from the wax that covers the seed. I recall having seen a row of the trees on a street in Jackson in November. The glowing wine-red leaves were still clinging to the branches and among them the white seeds in clusters of three. Birds come in flocks to eat them.

André Michaux is credited with bringing the tallow tree to Middleton Gardens in the late eighteenth century, along with the gingko and the Japanese varnish tree (*Firmiana simplex*), also called the Chinese parasol tree, the Chinese bottle tree, and the Phoenix tree. In Charleston it is called popcorn tree. It has escaped from gardens and grows all along the South Carolina coast, into the southeastern tip of North Carolina. I know of a tree that is growing on a street in Charlotte, and has even reseeded, but I cut down one that I planted against the south side of my house, as it was killed back so badly in severe winters. Mine never colored in the fall, perhaps because only certain forms do.

I asked Mrs. Netherland for permission to quote from her letters. "You may quote me if you wish in your book," she wrote. "A person who writes has my greatest respect. I enjoy my bulletin, and I have learned a lot about unusual plants. I also get a small glimpse of the people of my adopted state. (I am from Louisiana.) I must say that the impression I get is of a kind, gentle, hard-working people."

Mrs. Netherland's daughter-in-law lives in Hawaii, and sends her seeds of tropical plants, such as bird-of-paradise, ginger, and wood rose. "The bird-of-paradise and the ginger," Mrs. Netherland writes me, "will be kept indoors in winter, if I have luck with them. The wood rose will be planted in the spring and treated as an annual." The wood rose is a perennial morning glory, botanically *Merremia tuberosa*, with yellow flowers and wide, five- to seven-fingered leaves. Its name comes from the seedpods, which look like single-petaled roses carved out of smooth, brown wood.

*

Miss Voleene Martin started selling seeds in the 1960s. She sends them in the envelopes that have brought seeds to her. The postmarks cover the map from Grand Prairie, Texas, to Mariposa, California, to Flint, Michigan. Spelling doesn't seem to bother the mailman. One envelope was addressed to "Mrs. Volone Murton, Shinnon, Mississippi, in cair of Odell." I'd dearly love to know what came in all those envelopes. I sent Miss Voleene a picture, from a seed catalog, of Tithonia rotundifolia and asked if it was what she advertises as torch flower. She said yes. The tithonia sold in the trade as Torch is supposed to be a dwarf variety, but Miss Voleene's tithonias shot up to the usual height with flowers above my reach. I had not had tithonias in years, and I did enjoy their splash of scarlet in the fall. Even in November I picked the velvet flowers, like single dahlias, for the house. Plants from seed sown in May will bloom late in July or early in August, and on until frost.

Whenever I ordered seeds, Miss Voleene would put a note in with them: "I thank you, Miss Liz." But the last time I asked a question (whether her red fire plant is a celosia), she replied, in the stamped envelope I had enclosed, "I'm sorry I'm not much at reading strange hand writing—can't even make out your last name. But I do understand you want information concerning flowers, so am sending two addresses of seed catalogs so you may find out whatever you want to know." There was a postscript: "I hope you are interested in the Gospel too."

A copy of *The Herald of Truth* and one of *Gospel Minutes* were enclosed.

*

Mrs. Rhunella Johnson lives in Bay Springs, which is in Zone 8. I wrote her to ask her about the pink spider lily (*Lycoris squamigera*); the white spider lily, which might be a hymenocallis, but might as easily be the white form of the red spider lily (*Lycoris radiata*); and the feather hyacinth (*Muscari comosum*) 'Plumosum'. The feather hyacinth is now rare, but was once prized in old gardens. "Doubtless," Louise Beebe Wilder says, "it appealed to the Victorian taste." It is seldom found in the trade, but I had it once from an importer, and it bloomed for two Aprils before it disappeared. It was introduced into England from the South of France in 1596, and early came to enliven American gardens with its plumy blossoms, as translucent as blue-violet glass.

Mrs. Johnson wrote back:

> I received your order for the flower bulbs. Am so busy now gathering before frost hits that it will be a few weeks before I get them mailed, but you will receive them. Yes, pink spider lily is called surprise lily, and it does come up and bloom suddenly. The feather hyacinth is an old flower that has been in the family a long time. I don't know just how many years I have been advertising in the bulletin. My oldest child is twenty-one years old, and I started a long time before he was born. I am going to keep your letter, as I don't have time now to write you about all the flowers, and I can write later. My little two year old son is trying to help me write you.

*

Mrs. Brown calls her place Bessie's Ornamental Flower Garden. It is in Crystal Springs, also in Zone 8. Her feather-leaf fern, which came to me only slightly winter-worn at the end of one January, is dusty-miller, and her rose-that-lives-forever is *Sedum spectabile*, certainly one of the most satisfactory and ever-living of all perennials, with its clean gray, succulent foliage, and, in late summer, flat heads of dusty rose flowers. It is always cherished by the children, who like to make dolls' hot-water bottles out of the fleshy leaves, by skillfully detaching the skin of the underside from the midrib and inflating the leaf—a delicate operation.

Almost no one who advertises Texas bluebonnets, a favorite name in the bulletins, actually offers the gentian-blue lupines that are the state flower of Texas. Mrs. Brown is no exception. Her bluebonnet is spiderwort (*Tradescantia virginiana*). I suppose the triangular flower reminded some-one of a tricorne, and so became a bonnet. The blue of the flower is not as intense as that of the real Texas bluebonnet.

Mrs. Brown's "vine with red berries, climbs trees or brick," is *Euonymus radicans*. The form that grows around old houses, and is carried by the birds from garden to garden, never has scale, though every plant that I have ever had from a commercial source has been eaten up by it. In its juvenile state it is perfectly evergreen, and spreads over the ground rooting as it grows, making a close, low cover, but given a chance it climbs by aerial roots on whatever it comes in contact with. It never blooms in its juvenile state. In its adult state it stops climbing, becomes shrubby, and is no longer perfectly evergreen, although the foliage holds until severe weather and appears very early in the spring. The fruits are white pods from which the scarlet seeds dangle.

*

Sometimes the market bulletin plants are not for sale through the mail but must be called for:

Come to my place for pretty flowers cheap, have so many.

Will sacrifice all my yard and window plants at my place, have too many.

Come and bring your own spade, do your own digging.

Will give a large pink oleander to anyone who will haul it away and provide several buckets of good dirt to fill the hole.

In one issue of the bulletin, Miss Linnie Roberts of Crystal Springs offered to give plants to anyone who would come for them. "It was specifically stated," she wrote in a later issue, "that they were to be picked up at my house. As a result of this listing I have received hundreds of letters, checks, money, etc. It is impossible for me to answer these letters. Every penny of the money will be returned, but it may take weeks. I am sorry that I cannot mail the plants, and I hope everyone will understand."

In the exchange column there are offers to swap plants for other plants or for feed sacks. Feed sacks are in great demand, especially matching patterns, for making into skirts, blouses, and dresser covers. One issue includes the following offers:

All colors of mums (with nice roots), six false dragons, two St. Joseph's lilies, and one small gran-

dad greybeard, for two 100-pound feed sacks (print
or white) free of snags and mildew.

Watermelon-red crepe myrtle for pink crepe myrtle.
My plants are improved type, have real large blooms,
so large they weep like a weeping willow. I want the
same type, no small blooms. Will swap even. I don't
have money.

Another advertiser offered "anything I have, for three
wandering Jews."

*

The usual shrubs of country gardens appear in the market bulletins — flowering quince, snowball, rose-of-
Sharon, flowering almond, and winter honeysuckle, but
some of them have local names. The red flowering quince
is called fire bush or burning bush, in some parts of the
South, and mock orange (*Philadelphus*) is known as English
dogwood. A tame dogwood is one that comes out of a
garden, and a wild dogwood is one that has been collected. Various things are called spireas — there are popcorn, babybreath, button, snowdrop, and winter-flower-
ing spirea.

The names of some of the southern shrubs need no
explanation — pomegranate, oleander, gardenia — but
others are puzzling. The red magnolia is no magnolia,
though it is in the same family. It is *Illicium floridanum*, the
native anise tree, a small evergreen, ten feet tall or less,
that grows in swamps from Florida to Louisiana and is
said to be hardy to southern New Jersey. In my garden it
sometimes begins to bloom as early as mid-March and
stays in bloom for two months. The flowers are many-
petaled, oxblood red rosettes, something like sweet betsy,

but not sweet smelling. To the contrary, because of their unpleasant odor the red magnolia is sometimes called the wet-dog tree. But the flowers smell bad only at close quarters, and the leaves have a pleasant anise scent.

Red wisteria is a South American legume, *Sesbania punicea*, with fine, pale green foliage and short racemes of scarlet flowers. Naturalized along the Gulf Coast, it sometimes reseeds as far north as Charlotte. I should think it would make a good tub plant—as good a tub plant as *Cassia corymbosa*, which is used on northern terraces for summer bloom and then overwintered in cool but frost-free cellars. The farm women advertise this cassia as canary tree, for its bright yellow flowers set off by cool gray-green, willowy leaves.

Moss locust is the beautiful rose acacia, *Robinia hispida*, one of a number of different shrubs that may turn up in the market bulletins as rose-of-Sharon: "rooted rose of Sharon, looks like sweet peas, real pretty, blooms in spring." As it comes from the southern mountains, the rose acacia is hardy, but those who have not lived with it should be warned. It is as vicious as it is lovely, running in all directions and sending out innumerable suckers. When it blooms for me, at the end of April, I have not the heart to root it out, and then by fall I find out that it has taken over much of the garden.

Another legume of the Lower South is the bird-of-paradise, *Caesalpinia gilliesii*, a small and straggling shrub that might be groomed into shape for a tub plant. I have read that it is fetid, but I have never found the scent unpleasant. The flower is pale yellow, with long, trailing, red stamens like the tail of a tropical bird. The other bird-of-paradise advertised by the farm women is *Strelitzia reginae*, but I always know which one they mean, as the *Strelitzia* is much more expensive.

*

I asked Lula Gammill about the bird's-eye bush, which she advertised as "laden with small red berries in winter." She wrote me back that the bush "makes a lot of limbs and grows three feet tall. It has wine-purple berries thick on the stems. They are small and look like wax." I suspect this shrub to be *Symphoricarpos orbiculatus*. I also asked Miss Gammill about her blue spear lily. She said it is also called Indian hyacinth, and she will send me bulbs. I hope it will be *Camassia scilloides*, the little wild hyacinth that grows in meadows and along the sides of streams from Georgia to Texas, ranging as far north as Pennsylvania. In *Flowers Native to the Deep South*, Caroline Dorman describes it as having a tender stem, six to twelve inches high, that bears a spike of delicately scented, light blue flowers. She says it is found in rich, dry soil, in sun or semishade, and that it is ideal for the rock garden.

Mrs. Gammill grows lots of old-time flowers: lilac and flowering almond, the flowering quince (which she calls red hawthorn), and three spireas—the double snowdrop, the snowflake, and the bridal-wreath. Once she wrote me:

> I have the old fashion velvet rose already rooted and the everblooming pink rose and the red, an old fashion bright red rose, a white rose, and Paul's scarlet. I have the old fashion white iris and the purple we used to call flags, zinnias we used to call old maids, October pinks or chrysanthemums, and bachelor's buttons. . . . I may have other old fashion plants, but

I don't think of them now. . . . My father was born in Pickens County, South Carolina. That was a long time ago. He came to Mississippi, married my mother and never did go back. I am seventy-one years old.

It has been a long time since I have heard from Mrs. Gammill, and I haven't seen any of her advertisements recently. I wrote to tell her that I think of her often and would like to hear from her. I hoped that if she couldn't answer my letter herself, someone else would get it and answer for her. But I never heard.

*

In the column for "Plants Wanted," I once came across a request for some "old time plants—love-tangle (a vine) and the white star jessamine, the one with a small star flower that smells like sweet-gum not gardenia." I don't know what sweet gum smells like, though children used to gather it for chewing, but if the plant wanted has a musty odor it must be *Trachelospermum*. Star jessamine is a name used in the market bulletin for almost any small white, sweet-smelling flower: for the true jasmines, the various species of *Jasminum*, and for the Confederate jessamine, *Trachelospermum jasminoides*, the favorite flower of Jefferson Davis, who grew it in his garden at Beauvoir. It is a glossy, evergreen vine that grows and blooms, and even seeds itself, as far north as Charlotte. In the North it can be grown in a sunny window.

Love-entangled is an old name for nigella or love-in-a-mist, but as often happens when old names linger, the farm women have transferred it to another plant. Love-tangle vine is their name for Kenilworth ivy, an old favorite for hanging baskets.

Kenilworth ivy, incidentally, I have also seen advertised

as Kettleworth ivy. It often happens that as plants pass from the hands of one gardener to another, their names change in odd ways, through oral transmission. Some of these alterations in spelling when they are written down are: Eli Agnes for *Eleagnus*; the Festive Maxine peony for Festiva Maxima; Ellen Bouquet amaryllis for the rose-colored crinum, Ellen Bosanquet; Virginia's Philadelphia for *Philadelphus × virginalis*; rose-of-Charon; red star arise for red star-anise; and watery spirea for the spirea named Anthony Waterer. I am reminded of the gardener who asked me to come see her "wiggly rose," which turned out to be *Weigela florida*, and of another who called the rose Etoile de Hollande, Miss Estelle of Holland.

Reading the market bulletins is like walking through a country garden with sun on the flowers, in their very names: princess feather, four-o'clock, love-in-a-mist, bachelor's buttons, Joseph's coat, touch-me-not, kiss-me-at-the-garden-gate, ladyfingers, redbird bush, rainbow fairy, pink sunburst. Sometimes the names have a darker tone: devil's-shoestring, devil's-nip, devil's-walking-stick, graveyard moss, graveyard vine and a good many others with demonic or funereal names. I have never discovered what all of these are, but Mrs. Chrismon, who, in her little garden in Greensboro, North Carolina, has grown more kinds of plants than anyone I know, has supplied many of the missing Latin names:

> *Yucca filamentosa* grew in my grandmother's garden, and she called it devil's-shoestring. Jack-in-the-pulpit is devil's nip, and *Aralia spinosa* is devil's-walking-stick. Some call *Sedum sarmentosum* graveyard moss, and *Vinca minor* is graveyard vine. My daughter says they call fuchsia redbird bush in New Orleans. *Polygonum*

orientale is the plant known as ladyfingers, and I have heard it called kiss-me-at-the-garden-gate, but more commonly it is called princess feather.

Prince's-feather is Parkinson's name for London Pride, *Saxifraga umbrosa*, and also, in England, for *Amaranthus hybridus erythrostachys*, but in America it is a common name, as Mrs. Chrismon mentioned, for *Polygonum orientale*, an annual knotweed native to Asia and naturalized in this country. To complete the confusion involved with all common names, no matter how poetic they are, in England the common lilac is sometimes called prince's-feather—or sometimes, as in John Clare's poem, prissy-feathered tree:

Her bonny white straw bonnet
Was sweet and fair to see;
White flowered ribbons danced upon it
Like the prissy-feathered tree.

As a flower name, princess-feather must have come to this country with John Brickell, who in 1737 gave the flowers in the bogs of North Carolina English names: "Pleasant and delightful Savannahs or Meddows with their Green Liveries interwoven with various kinds of beautiful Color and fragrant Odours which several seasons afford. They appear at a distance like so many Pleasure Gardens being such as Tulip, Trumpet-flower and Princess feather."

In the South, as one of its common names indicates, *Vinca minor* is often found in old cemeteries, an association that goes back to the ancient custom of crowning prisoners on their way to execution with garlands of periwinkle. They called it the flower-of-death. In *Old Time*

Gardens, Alice Morse Earle says it has always been a flower of mystery; the French name is *violette des Sorcier*, but she likes to call it by another ancient name, joy-of-the-ground. Besides *Sedum sarmentosum*, another plant, in the North Carolina mountains at least, is known and grown as graveyard moss. It is *Euphorbia cyparissias*, which has become naturalized from Europe, grows in waste places from Massachusetts to Virginia to Colorado, and has accumulated various folk names, such as kiss-me-dick, welcome-to-our-house, and Bonaparte's crown.

In the South, thrift is not *Armeria* but *Phlox subulata*. False dragons are *Physostegia virginiana*. June bells, "purple, bloom all summer," are *Campanula rapunculoides*, the rover bellflower, so named for reasons anyone who has ever grown it will understand perfectly. Grandfather's whiskers, my mother learned when she once sent a quarter to find out what they were, are cleome. She got six little wilted plants wrapped in newspaper and a note written in pencil: "Dear Flower Friend: I hope you will enjoy these plants. Let me know how they do." She did not begrudge the old lady her pin money, but careless packing is not always so easily forgiven. The editor of the bulletin asks "to be notified of evidence of bad faith on the part of any advertiser." Plants are often advertised as "damp packed" or "wrapped to live," and for the most part they arrive in good condition.

Not everyone who advertises plants in the market bulletin is a farm woman; there is also Mr. Kimery. My correspondence with him began with the wisteria vine. He wrote:

> Thank you for your order. The wisteria vine may not come up until spring. If it don't come up, let me

know, and I will send you another free. It blooms in June, or mine does, long white blooms, about four inches. I'll write you a letter in a few days and tell you about what I have got, and a little about myself. Thanks again, and I hope you luck with all your flowers.

When he sent the list he promised, he enclosed a sheaf of colored pictures cut out of plant catalogs to identify some of his offerings.

I have plenty of all, but I am out of the tuberose. You will know all about them. If you want anything I have almost all kinds of bulbs, plants and shrubs. I'll be glad to help you. I have about one acre of flowers. It keeps me busy at time to keep them clean, but I have loved flowers all my life. Oh yes, my mother said when I was large enough to crawl, she would have to go out and get me out of the hot sun. Ha. I have been in the flower business about thirty years; have mailed orders to every state in the U.S.

Along with the colored pictures, he enclosed two paper cutouts. On one was printed "Kim's hand at six months," on the other "Kim's foot at six months."

Mr. Kimery's post office is in Saulsbury, Tennessee, but his acre, Hilltop Nursery, is over the line in Mississippi. In 1970 his wife died. "I am staying at home," he wrote, "and I am making it just fine, but it will never be the same." He has brothers and sisters and two sons living nearby, and a daughter in Oregon. He flew there on a jet for a visit. One of his sisters is the alto in a quartet of gospel singers.

Mr. Kimery is the tenor. "We are on the go a lot of the time," he wrote, "and we enjoy it. We have some beautiful songs on a record. We went to Memphis to make it." I asked if it was for sale. It was, and at a discount to flower friends. When I found "The Church in the Wildwood" among the hymns, I thought of *Losing Battles*:

> Oh come—come—come—come the bass voice of Uncle Noah Webster started, and they came in with "Come to the church in the wild wood, oh come to the church in the dell."

I sent another record to Eudora. "I love the way they all 'come,'" she wrote, "especially his sister. I only wish they had had enough room to give all the verses. You get the very air in the room, and the smell of the country flowers—I expect zinnias and gladiolus and salvia in a tub—and the warm day. It's all so expressive and Sunday-like. How did you and Mr. Kimery intersect on Gospel by way of flowers?" I told her that it happened because she had put my name on the mailing list of the bulletin some thirty years ago.

I asked Mr. Kimery about some of the names on his plant list: Chinese hollyhock (striped flowers), cat-bells, spider legs, sensitive vine, and the yellow rose of Texas. When I wrote, a little striped mallow that I had been trying to name for some time was in bloom, so I sent a flower and asked whether it was the Chinese hollyhock. It was. It is a biennial, but it reseeds itself indefinitely. I am always coming on it in old gardens, but no commercial seed companies seem to list it, despite its attractive pink blossoms with lavender stripes and its resistance to heat and drought. Later, Dr. Solymosy identified it as *Malva sylvestris*, a native of Europe that has become naturalized in this country. Park Seed sells this as *Malva alcea* 'zebrina'. Its medicinal uses are no longer taken seriously, but in earlier times all parts were used for various ills, the root, Culpeper said in his *Complete Herbal and English Physician*, having the most virtue.

The cat-bell, Mr. Kimery said, "was called that name years ago by old people; they said the Indians called them cat-bells. They have small seeds in black pods, and when you shake them they sound like little bells. The kids around here play with them. This is all I know to tell you." He added a postscript: "I sure have mailed a lot of cat-bells." In Caroline Dorman's *Flowers Native to the Deep South* I found that this small, insignificant wild flower is *Crotalaria sagittalis*. This specific name, though not listed in *Hortus Third*, came from the conspicuous stipules, shaped like arrowheads and pointing down the stem.

Spider legs was Mr. Kimery's name for cleome, and a very good one to describe its dangling seed pods. The usual name, spider flower, is not at all appropriate for the delicate orchid-like blossoms. Four color forms of *Cleome hasslerana* are listed in Park's catalog, as well as the yellow-flowered *Cleome lutea*, which as I had it in my former garden in Raleigh was not worth growing. Pink Queen, which is pink and white, is the one grown most often. There is a Purple Queen and a Rose Giant. The most beautiful of all is Helen Campbell with its very large, airy heads of pure white. Although they droop in the midday sun, these cool flowers are a blessing to midsummer borders in the morning and the evening.

The sensitive vine is the sensitive brier, a thorny vining legume that trails on the ground. Mr. Kimery says it is called shame vine because it will close up when touched. The flowers are like those of its relative, the mimosa, little pink balls of fluff, and they have the fragrance of hyacinths. About this plant, which can be one of two closely related native American species, either *Schrankia microphylla* or *S. nuttallii*, Mrs. Lounsberry says that the mountaineer who steps on it with bare feet in a sandy meadow is unlikely to appreciate its beauty, "but to the well shod it is one of the sweetest and most unique personalities of all native plants."

"The rose of Texas," Mr. Kimery wrote, "is double yellow. I sent you all I have. They will live. Hope so." I hope so too, for one I got earlier died before I had a chance to tell anything about it except that its thorns were sharp and numerous, which made me think it was the old brier, Harison's Yellow (1830), common in gardens and of American origin. The yellow rose of Texas appears often in the market bulletins, but sometimes it is not a rose at all but double kerria (*Kerria japonica*).

Mr. Kimery lives so peacefully on his hilltop, with his flowers and trips to Memphis with the quartet, that I forgot that there is violence in the world. One of his letters startled me out of this illusion.

Just to let you know what happened here, Wednesday night someone put some kind of bomb in my mailbox and some more. So last night a man watched his, and he caught them. So the law is holding them, and the FBI will come from Memphis tomorrow and get them. They have been doing that for two years, but they are going where they can't do it anymore. If you ever want any flowers let me know. I have so many of such a lot of things. I can let you have them cheap.

Ain't this world getting in a sinful mess? Everything from that Watergate to raping and killing. Memphis is so mean. We don't know when we go to bed at night if someone will come in and kill us for a dime. They never think about hereafter, or don't care.

I think about Mr. Kimery, about all who sell their seeds and plants through the market bulletin. And I care.

Dooly Yams and Indian Peaches

The bulletins offer seeds of vegetables and fruits as well as flowers. They are measured by the teaspoon or tablespoon (level or heaping), by the box (snuff box, match box, soda box), or by the teacup: "Fresh choice seeds, choice varieties, can be planted now through fall, half cup 30 cents plus stamped envelope."

The vegetables are mostly local and old timey: little white lady or rice cowpeas, little brown running cowpeas, whipperwill cowpeas; old-fashion freeze-proof winter turnip seed; white sugar crowders and six-week, purple hull, fall cowpeas; old time Dooly yams and Gold Rush sweet potatoes; cowhorn okra; little icebox corn (not sweet corn), June corn, Indian corn; running white willowleaf butterbean; Black Beauty eggplants. Advertisements for little old-timey red tomato seeds appear regularly in spring and fall, along with seeds of bouquet peppers and long green pickling cucumbers.

The fruits are local too: old-fashioned summer pears

and sugar pears; old-fashioned apples; old-time Indian peaches. If planted before the last of December, "clear-seed or freestone seed from non-grafted peach trees will come up next spring and will bear fruit when two years old. Peaches ripen in July and August."

I wonder whether the "floral peach bush, brought from Korea by a GI, perfectly hardy, grows four feet high and bears white-fleshed freestone fruit" might not be the Chinese dwarf peach from which the Bonanza peach, a recently introduced variety highly touted by nurseries for home planting, is said to have been developed. It is reported to thrive wherever peaches ordinarily grow, and in ten years an unpruned bush will probably be only five or six feet high.

What is advertised as "old fashion pomegranate" will not be *Punica granatum*, even though in much of the South *P. granatum* is a highly rewarding shrub for its narrow, glossy leaves, evergreen in a mild winter, its blossoms that combine wax and fluff, and the fruits that follow —complicated in structure but delightful in their tartness for the persistent. In country gardens all over the South the little sweet-smelling melon, *Cucumis melo Dudaim*, is called pomegranate. Though edible, it is grown for its fragrance. The English call it Queen Anne's pocket melon. One of my old friends in Mississippi says she used to wrap the little melon in her handkerchief, when she was a school girl, and put it in the pocket of her pinafore. The small, spicy, cinnamon-and-yellow striped balls are a convenient size for a pocket, and some people still keep them in closets to perfume them. I have been told that the Dudaim is called vine peach in the North, but what the market bulletin calls vine peach is (I think)

Cucumis melo Chito, the mango melon or lemon cucumber, available from Park. Liberty Hyde Bailey says in *The Garden of Gourds* that it is used for pickling as well as for ornament, but is not as showy as the Dudaim. One advertiser who offers seeds of this vine peach in the bulletin says it grows abundant peaches that "make fine preserves for home use; also fine to feed hogs. Recipes for preserves and pickles will accompany seeds."

Not surprisingly, the bulletin also lays before its readers watermelon seeds, in great variety: golden honey, Stone Mountain, black diamond, rattlesnake, and icecream watermelons praised for being "pure, sweet, and juicy" with "gray rind and yellow meat."

In September, the plants of Pocahontas strawberries appear: "Now is the time to put them out for early berries next spring. Also, tree-type everbearing blackberries, ripen last of April through May." Cuttings of the brown turkey fig are offered in the fall, as are "old time rooted scuppernong vines, ready to set out."

An advertiser in Gulfport offers "grafted Japan persimmons; kumquat plants, large sweet fruit. Never had any to freeze." Sugar cane is in good supply: "Six different kinds of Louisiana sugar cane for seed or chewing; red, green, and ribbon, hard or soft." "Old time gooseneck sorgum seed." "Honey drip sorghum seed."

Japanese Silkies, July Dogs, and Paint Horses

The livestock columns of the *Mississippi Farm Bulletin* are as varied and as colorful as the plant material. In the poultry section, Japanese silkies and bearded white Polish bantams appear. Eggs are exchanged: "I believe I have one of the purest strains of old Southern Roundhead games in existence today, will swap eggs for any purebred strain of fancy bantam eggs." There are peacocks (a "snow white male with eight foot tail"), silver and golden and ring-necked pheasants, and pigeons. The pigeons are mostly giant homers, racing homers, and Birmingham rollers. A homer is a homing pigeon; rollers are sporting pigeons, which flip over as they fly through the air. A breeder offers pigeons in "twenty-five varieties, utility and fancy, with a special to Boy Scouts for winning Merit Badges." I feel for those pigeons who go to the Scouts. I know a dog who won a merit badge for a Scout, and it didn't find it easy.

Mules, horses, and burros; home-raised horse mule; male burro, ideal pet; work horses, walking horses, riding horses, trotting horses, using horses. . . . "Must sell my favorite using horses, as my ranch has been sold; both of excellent breeding and well trained, young and sound, spirited but gentle. Will sell only to good homes and excellent riders who can appreciate their quality." "Paint horse, very gentle, rides and works to collar." "One year old quarter horse colt, iron red color, has been handled a little, will not lead out good yet, but is halter broke." A nice pony is offered for a cow, and a sorrel saddle horse for "a horse or mule that an aged man can plow—no jumper or saddle fighter." And Sally Perry wants to sell her black mare: "has no one to handle her."

The dogs are best of all. Almost any breed that is recognized by the American Kennel Club will turn up—and many that are not.

Collies are "kind to children, and good to bark around

the house." Fox terriers are squirrel dogs: "puppies from good squirrel stock, weaned, wormed, and eating well." There is a hound for every use. Beagles are good on rabbits. A "young beagle trained on rabbits has a dandy mouth and is fast on game; account for selling, too close to highway." Another is described as of "slow speed, but good for trials. Reason for selling, too slow for owner's pack."

Tree hounds are classed by color instead of blood strains. They are blueticks, black-and-tans, and redbones. Black-and-tans are coon, possum, and squirrel dogs. One female is described as a coon and possum dog at night, and a top squirrel dog in day time. Another will "run and tree well, has no bad habits, and will take to water." Another "cannot tree but is a good strike dog, runs coon and wildcats." Two puppies are advertised as "fat and healthy and starting to run; their ears lap around their noses." Redbone hounds are advertised as "wide, fast, delux strike dogs," running everything from squirrels to wild hogs.

A curious ad I found in the bulletin requires a bit of explanation. A man wanted a cur, but said, "If he is not a full-blooded cur, please do not write." Originally the name cur was applied to a watchdog or a sheepdog without any reference to low breeding. "This Cur dog . . . will serve my sheep to gather." (Spenser, 1591.) But there are mixtures of cur and other breeds, cur dogs in the other sense of the word. "Two male puppies 6 months old, ready to hunt this fall. Mother is Boston bull, father large cur." Mixed blood seems to be not only acceptable but also desirable, if the strains are good. "Two puppies, beginning to run; mother is black and tan coon dog,

daddy is half black and tan, other half bloodhound."
"Pair of puppies, half redbone, half bluetick, good size,
stout, able to go, will make good dogs for anything."

When I came across these puppies for sale—"blue
leopards, all have two glass eyes, sire of pups good cow
dog, dam works some, is brown with black spots and has
glass eyes"—I asked Caroline Dormon what in the world
a glass-eyed dog could be. She said it must be a Catahoula
hound.

"These dogs are unmistakable," she said. "They have a
strange bluish cast, numerous spots of different colors,
and they always have blue eyes."

No one knows the origin of these dogs, but I once
read in the bulletin that the breed was developed to find
and trail wild cattle and that a good dog of this kind
should be able to trail and hold a six-hundred-pound
hog. Caroline says that they were once used to round up
the droves of half-wild hogs that lived in the Catahoula
swamps, and that they were ferocious fighters. Highly
intelligent, these dogs lured hogs into pens by running in
themselves and then quickly leaping out; then the hogs
would be closed in.

July dogs are foxhounds, but they also run deer. I puzzled over the name for a long time before I read in Fred
Streever's *The American Trail Hound* that they are the prog-
eny of a celebrated hound called Old July, a descendant
of Mountain and Muse, a pair of Irish hounds imported
into Maryland in 1814.

In the exchange columns dogs change hands. Gregory
Taylor of Buckatunna wanted to swap "two mixed
hounds, bobcat and deer dogs, for any kind of tree dog
that will stay treed." A "real good cattle dog" is offered

for "some laying hens (about twenty-five)," and a "heavy, long-eared, six months old beagle out of good blooded, hard-hunting stock" for "some homemade preserves or home cured meat."

Dog lovers use the market bulletins to inquire for pets to be had for nothing. Wanted: "To get in touch with someone who has a Chihuahua dog to give away. I have an asthma victim in my home, and have been advised to get him a little Chihuahua dog and he would get better." Wanted: "If you have a bird dog puppy that is killing chickens or is gun shy, and you are going to get rid of him, please do not kill him, I want him." In the pages of the market bulletin, many strange and wonderful things turn up, including human mercy and tenderness towards one another and towards beasts.

Under Fence and Close to Church

In the for sale columns most anything can be found, from a horse-drawn sorghum mill to an old, historic plantation house just off the Natchez Trace. Farms are featured as having plenty of shade trees, a river running across the place, a good well of water on the back porch; as being under fence and close to church, with good hunting and fishing.

Dinner and plantation bells are advertised, and wash pots of all sizes. An invalid in a wheelchair advertises for "white broom sage brooms" (broom sedge). She says she wants a regular supply, as she cannot sweep very well with stick brooms. Turkey wings, barred or white, tom or hen, are sold for crumbing the table or sweeping the

hearth. Feather beds and pillows and fluffy goosefeathers
are for sale, used or unused. "Clean feather bed, never
used in any kind of sickness." "Am selling all my pillows,
am allergic to feathers." Beeswax, bee equipment, bees
are offered, as is honey—fresh honey, bright or dark,
chunk, comb or strained; honey sold in ten pound pails,
postpaid, and honey "you come get, bring your jugs."
Fifty-pound cans of very fresh, home-cooked lard are for
sale, and clean white mutton tallow. Sun-dried fruits of
various kinds are offered—especially apples, "nice, bright,
old time summer red apples." Pecans can be bought
shelled or unshelled, or the buyer may gather them by
the hamper, truck, or car load. Black walnuts are also
available, and peanuts: little dark red peanuts, small size
bunch peanuts, and Spanish peanuts. Then there are
chufas, small tubers of the yellow nut sedge (*Cyperus
esculentus sativus*) also called earth-almonds, that are eaten
when dry or fed to pigs and chickens. Gourds and gourd
seeds are in good supply: the bushel basket kind, "can
make many pretty and useful things out of them"; the
kind that are used for martin and bluebird houses; the
kind that are used for minnow buckets; and also vase,
dipper, dishrag, and swan-neck gourds.

One of the oddments that appear on occasion is corn
beads or "Indian beads for stringing on string," as they
were described in an advertisement by Mrs. W. L. Null,
who wrote me in response to my inquiry:

> Concerning the bead seed, yes, I grow them. When
> they come up they look just like corn, and will sucker
> out from the mother stalk. They do not make a
> bloom. Later on you will notice beads in the buds of

the limbs all over the bush. When they turn brown it is time to gather them and spread them out before stringing. Some call them corn beads as the stalks look so much like corn, but the true name is Indian beads as the Indians raised them and wore them. I hope I have been of some help to you. Write me again, if you care to, if I can help you in any way.

She signed herself "A Friend."

Indian beads are listed in the Park catalog as Job's-tears, *Coix lacryma-jobi*, but they are also called Juno's-tears. They are said to be magic. This annual grass is very popular in the South. Mrs. Null once wrote me that she thinks the beads are pretty when dyed, but I like their natural colors: tones of buff and beige, and from pearl gray to the darkness of a thunder cloud—all as beautiful as fine enamel. As Mrs. Null so closely observed, there are no real flowers: the stamens and the pistil are inside the bead and project through a hole in the top. *Coix lacryma-jobi* is grown for food in India and for medicine in China.

In the early December market bulletins, there are always advertisements for berries and evergreens for Christmas decorations: "holly limbs with lots of red berries, cedar branches with blue berries, magnolia leaves, spruce pine leaves, and running vine-leaf like bamboo with orange and red berries; in each box will be a big size red Christmas stocking and two large pine cones." Dried material is sent out in shoe boxes: small, buff-colored chinquapin burs; tiny, dark, delicately fashioned alder cones; the slender, cinnamon-colored capsules of the tulip tree; pods, sprays, sedges, and grasses in faded tones of sherry and umber and burnt sienna. Sometimes I find familiar things like sycamore balls and mimosa pods in the boxes;

or a curiously wrought fruit-spray, as bleached as if it had been at the bottom of the sea; or small, square mahogany beads that seem to be strung on thin wire.

One fall I had some correspondence with Mrs. Radau, who collects such things from the woods and fields of her river plantation near Saucier and sends them all over the country. She wrote:

> Now that the new baby and the twins have got over whooping cough, I shall be able to fill orders promptly. Most of my pods and cones are from native trees, and I put in seed sprays of dockweed and pods of okra and hibiscus. I also collect seeds of rare native trees and shrubs, such as *Stewartia malacodendron*, *Magnolia pyramidata*, *Illicium floridanum*, witch hazel, and our beautiful silver-bell (*Halesia*).

Mrs. Radau shares my constant concern for knowing the scientific names of plants, as well as their common or folk names. When she wants to know what something is, she sends specimens to the University of Southwestern Louisiana for identification.

No Objection to Snuff

In the employment columns whole families are being sought for, or are seeking, work. A man with a wife and six children, four large enough to work, wants any kind of job on a farm. A large family is wanted to work cotton and help milk forty cows. A farmer offers a comfortable home to a small family of cotton pickers, but, he says, "People who live here must be happy." All must be sober, honest, and reliable. Drinking is not tolerated, but there is no objection to snuff. A beekeeper is needed who must not be afraid of bees or work; wages will be determined on worth. An elderly man is wanted for gardening, repairs, and poultry work—no objection to a handicap. A young man wants a job on a farm taking care of an elderly couple and doing chores. He likes people, likes to hunt and fish, is single, and does not run around much or get into mischief. He wants a place like home and will consider any job where he can receive a salary and perhaps raise a calf or two to sell.

Many advertisers are middle-aged or old people, looking for companionship or a home. A man wants "to retire like they used to before the war." He says he is easy to get along with, and he's looking for a home with someone needing help. A woman who wants a man to help out about the place will provide him with a cabin within a few feet of a fishing pond. A widow living alone wants a female companion. She will provide room, board, and TV. "No salary offered, no work expected."

*

I suppose I could have survived over the years without the *Mississippi Market Bulletin*; without letters to and from people like Mr. Kimery and Mrs. Breland; without the packages of sometimes mysterious seeds and plants from those southern country gardens; without the occasional insights into the lives of other people, with their sorrows but always with their joy in gardening. But my own life would have been a bit poorer without these things, for which I will always thank Eudora Welty. The poorly printed, cheap pulp pages of these market bulletins pulse with the very stuff of life.

The North Carolina Agricultural Review

For southeastern gardeners, the *North Carolina Agricultural Review* is a fine source of a great variety of native plant material, ranging from the balsam fir forests of the high mountains to the lowlands of the Atlantic Coast, from Sapphire Valley to Leland. Sapphire Valley is not on the map, but it has a zip code, and is in the mountains around Lake Sapphire. Leland is a community in Brunswick County, near Wilmington, North Carolina. From Sapphire Valley, Mrs. Beatrice Williams advertises American holly, mountain laurel, white pine, Canadian hemlock, and trailing arbutus. From Leland, Mrs. Bertha Little has a permit (No. 1143) to sell the Venus flytrap (*Dionaea muscipula*), an endemic of the Carolinas that is plentiful within a seventy-five-mile radius of Wilmington and ranges as far south as Charleston. Darwin called the flytrap the most wonderful plant in the world. Insects lighting on the twin blades of the modified leaves trigger springs that snap them together, to catch and consume their prey (even moderate-sized grasshoppers). The plant grows in pocosins and semibogs, where the soil is never very wet and never very dry. In May the umbels of frail white flowers stand well above the basal rosette.

*

In our mountains, the greatest number of native wild flowers are advertised by people who have lived for generations on Route 3, fourteen miles from Banner Elk, a town in Avery County near the Tennessee border. The one regular advertiser I've come to know best is Mrs. Ray Hicks.

Some time back, Mrs. Hicks sent me a handwritten list of more than sixty native species that she grows on her place. More were available, she said, but she couldn't always remember to put down everything. At her request, I sent her my first order early in the year, as she needed to know what I wanted before the time came to dig. We began to correspond, and since Mrs. Hicks always wrote "Dear Elizabeth," a mountain custom, I asked to call her Rosa. Her full name is Rosa Violet, which is most fitting. "Dear Elizabeth," she wrote me on the last day of February, 1975.

> I have been a while answering your letter, as we are getting over the flu. Granny is in the hospital real bad. I just expect to hear anything. We are having our winter now. Today has been a wonderful day, but it can change so fast. We have had plenty of water. Our roads have gone down in places, and our mail doesn't run too good when the roads are bad, but I think I can get you some of what you want of what I have. I haven't been out since I got sick, but I hope to get things off in April.

One sunny morning early that July, while I was staying with my friends the Hechenbleikners on Grandfather Mountain, Martha Hechenbleikner drove me to Banner Elk. There we stopped at a service station to ask our way to Rosa's and had no trouble getting directions: everyone knew Ray Hicks. We drove along Shawneehaw Creek to Blueberry Farm with its trim cornfields and orchards and the mountains blue in the distance, and turned onto Gwaltney Road, which runs into Wautaga County and on through Pisgah National Forest. All along the roadside, daisies, chicory, black-eyed susans, butterfly weed, and sunflowers were in bloom, and on shady banks scarlet bergamot, the tall, white spires of black cohosh, and *Viburnum cassinoides*, which the mountain people call shawneehaw, withe-rod, and wild raisin for its edible dark blue fruit.

After crossing the northern boundary line of Pisgah Forest, we came to the last turn. There beside the mail box we found Mr. Ray Hicks himself and his two sons. I had written to say we were coming but hadn't said when, and I don't know how long he had been standing there, watching for us to pull up in the car. The Hicks's house is on a narrow, dead-end road on the side of Rocky Knob, at an altitude of 4,200 feet. Behind it, there is a sheer drop of 2,000 feet to the Wautaga River. Beyond the river lies a chain of distant mountains on the line between North Carolina and Tennessee.

As we entered the house, Mr. Hicks called, "Here's your friend!" Rosa and Granny — who was cheerful, loving, and wheezing like a kettle about to boil, but hale and hearty except for asthma — came into the living room to greet us, and we sat down to talk like old friends, which Rosa's letters made me feel we were. After meeting those three stalwart mountain men, waiting so patiently on the hot and dusty roadside by the mailbox, Rosa was a surprise: so slight and slender, so dainty in her fresh cotton print, it was hard to believe that she was the mother of those two strapping young men or that she scrubbed on the scrubbing board all of those mudstained overalls. But her fragile appearance was deceptive. Rosa Hicks has the strength of her mountain heritage and a vitality of her own. Quick to sorrow, quick to mirth, she has a light in her dark eyes.

Granny is Ray Hicks's mother, Mrs. Nathan Hicks. The two grown sons and the youngest daughter, Juanita, made up the household. Two older daughters had married and gone to live in Tennessee.

Mr. Hicks had spent his life in the woods and fields gathering herbs and roots and barks to sell to the wholesale drug companies. His family has lived on Rocky Knob for generations, and he has a great store of mountain lore. His father, he says, was an orphan child who lived with his grandfather, who built the house. His father's great-grandfather, who is buried down by the Wautaga River, lived in a log cabin.

Rosa calls her flowers by their mountain names, but she uses *Wild Flowers of North Carolina*, by Justice and Bell, to identify them. By referring to Dr. Justice's photographs, when we wrote to one another, we could match the local names with the Latin ones.

Rosa's flower garden is a bank between the road and the lawn, with no paths between the plants. "You can travel there," she said, "without hurting anything." But the slope was so steep that I couldn't penetrate the upper reaches even with the aid of my cane. Summer flowers were in full bloom on that July day when Martha and I were there, and the colorful bank looked like an English herbaceous border. I saw the musk mallow, *Malva moschata*, for the first time. It is a European and North African perennial that has escaped from old gardens and become naturalized in meadows and along roadsides from North Carolina to Canada. The plants are bushy, about two feet tall, and covered with fragrant flowers of a clear and glowing but delicate pink with faint lines of a deeper rose, like those of *Malva sylvestris* in size and shape, but more effective in the garden. There is scant reference to this lovely plant in garden literature, except by Miss Jekyll, who liked to plant pink mallows with steel-blue sea holly, *Eryngium maritimum*. Also in bloom in Rosa's garden was *Linaria vulgaris*, commonly called butter-and-eggs. This little European toadflax (because someone thought that the flowers look like toads, or perhaps that the plants attracted toads), seldom found in nurseries, has escaped to our roadsides from the gardens where few Americans now grow it, thinking it too invasive, but in England it has always been appreciated. In Rosa's garden I also admired her wild raspberry, *Rubus odoratus*. It used to bloom in deep shade in my Raleigh garden, from May into July, but never freely. In the South, it thrives only in the mountains. The magenta flowers are like wild roses, the leaves three- to five-lobed, like maples. It is unarmed, only the fruits being like those of brambles, and the berries, which may ripen as late as September and can appear simultaneously with flowers, are delicious.

It was a good day, the day I finally met Rosa Hicks, and I wrote her right away to say so and to send her some sedum and to ask about some of the other sedums on her list, as well as hedyotis, saxifrages, and meadow rues.

"Been slow in answering your letter," she wrote on the twelfth of August. "We are in the canning rush. Good to see the jars fill up, but having trouble getting lids. I decided to take time now to answer. The white sedum is like the one on the top of page eighty-one."

This white sedum is *Sedum ternatum*, a native of rich woods in the mountains and piedmont of the Carolinas. I first saw it on a mountainside in Buncombe County, along the rocky banks of Reems Creek. It flourished in my Raleigh garden under the oak trees, but I could never get it established under the pines in Charlotte. Now Rosa has sent me a nice clump, and I hope this time it will take hold. It blooms in April, with the white flower heads and also the little round leaves in threes. I had sent Rosa *S. sarmentosum*, a yellow-flowered Chinese species and also *S. acre*, which the early herbalists called wall-pepper because of the sharp taste of its leaves and which English cottagers, for reasons I can't quite fathom, call welcome-home-husband-though-never-so-drunk.

The hedyotis, Rosa says, is not the familiar bluet (once *Houstonia caerulea*, now *Hedyotis caerulea*) that stars the spring woods, but the mountain bluet (*H. purpurea*), whose blossoms are not at all blue, but delicate pink. In the garden it is apt to be weedy, but as I saw it one April at the foot of Morrow Mountain, growing along a small, clear stream with *Oxalis violacea* and *Hieracium venosum*, it was dainty enough for an Alpine garden. A southern species, it ranges from Maryland to Georgia and Alabama.

Rosa's saxifrage is mountain lettuce, the *Saxifraga micranthidifolia* of Justice and Bell's *Wild Flowers of North*

Carolina. It has large, thin, light green leaves up to a foot long and panicles of small, white flowers in early summer. And Rosa says two species of meadow rue grow on the mountain, but she doesn't know which they are. One is probably *Thalictrum revolutum*, one of several tall ones that occur in the mountains. I grow another of the tall sorts in my garden, *T. polygamum*, which has narrow leaflets with pointed lobes and produces myriads of tiny, white flowers, like a spray of water, in July. The plant grows to eight feet and flops unless staked.

When I sent another list of questions to Rosa in mid-August, she wrote, "See if I can answer you earlier than I did your last letter. If I don't I'll probably be in another canning round. About the waterleaf, the leaves are like those of the one on page 158 of the Justice book, *Hydrophyllum virginianum*. I just went to check mine, but it had died back or the menfolk had cut it down." Waterleaf is often called Shawnee salad, for its tender, young shoots were eaten by various tribes of American Indians.

In November, Granny died, and Juanita Hicks went to Tennessee to visit her sister and look for a job. "Now I have more to do," Rosa wrote, "and will have to get used to doing things by myself again. Maybe my work will be so I don't have to be on the trot all the time. Maybe when you write again, I will have more time to answer. Well, I have more letters to write so I better get a move on me. Some people are easier to write to than others."

Early in the new year, when it was too cold to work outside and too cold inside to do anything but sit by the fire, Rosa made a list of all the plants in the Justice and Bell book that grow on her mountainside. There were seventy-three—and she listed many others that were not in the book. "Sitting inside looking out today, it's lovely outside," she wrote on the twelfth of February. "It has been cold and windy and a little snowy. We had up to six inches of snow, and there's still some of it around. A while back I took a peep at the flowers and noticed crocuses and snowdrops peeping up; was thinking of taking a peep today, but haven't got that far. Might be something else today, but I don't think so, because we have had too cold weather, and the ground has been frozen deep."

On the seventh of April, she wrote about the first wildflowers, "A pretty day—well, has been all week, but nights are frosty. Maybe that will help things and keep them tough and not so easy to get killed. I haven't noticed anything hurt by the freezing nights we had a while back. I haven't been in the woods to see what may be in bloom, but near the house the spring beauties, blood-root, hepatica, and the round-leafed yellow violet are out. When I can find the halberd-leafed violet I will send you one—might be next week if nothing happens."

Spring-beauty (*Claytonia virginica*) has another charming name, good-morning-spring. I thought of that when I found it one St. Valentine's day blooming under oak trees on the campus of the University of Mississippi, covering the ground like grass, although it doesn't take the place of turf, since the leaves disappear when the flowers fade. In Mrs. Dana's day there were great patches of spring-beauty along the carriage drive in Central Park. "One is always glad to discover these country children within our city limits," she wrote, "where they can be known and loved by those other children who are not so fortunate." My earliest date for this plant is the first week in March, and that year it went on blooming until mid-April. The petals are white or flesh-colored, with hairline veins that vary from the palest pink to the deepest rose. But the claytonia that Rosa grows is not C. *virginica*. It is C. *caroliniana*, an endemic of the southern Alleghanies from Virginia to Georgia, occurring in North Carolina only in the mountains along the Tennessee line. It differs from C. *virginica* only in having wider leaves and fewer flowers and blooming a little later.

My earliest date for bloodroot (*Sanguinaria canadensis*) is the twenty-second of February, and its bloom was as brief as it was beautiful. I have a splendid form of it that came to me from a nursery in the roots of some other plant. The flowers have twelve gleaming white petals, and they are nearly three inches across. Each bud comes up wrapped in a gray-green leaf and rises above it as the flower opens. As the flowers fade, the leaves grow taller. In 1735, when John Custis of Williamsburg sent bloodroot to Peter Collinson in London, Collinson said he had "3 sorts of pecoone" in his garden, "one with a small flower, one with a large flower, one with a double flower," adding politely, "but I was glad of yours, perhaps it may prove a variety." Puccoon is an Indian name, shortened in Appalachia to coon root. Years ago I had the double variety, flore-pleno, praised in a catalog as "a rarity of unsurpassed beauty," and I ordered it. It was puny and did not persist. A pink form I sent for proved to be dingy white with a wine tinge on the reverse of the petals. Thomas Jefferson commented in his *Garden Book* on the ephemeral bloom of bloodroot at Shadwell in 1766: "April 6, Narcissus and Puckoon open; April 13, Puckoon flowers fallen." Looking over my own records I find that in some exceptional years I have had bloodroots last two or three weeks.

Rosa's hepatica is H. *acutiloba*, the only one found in the high mountains of North Carolina. Its habitat is the Appalachians from Maine to northern Georgia. The flowers are usually white, but they are sometimes tinted with blue-violet or pink. The ones I had in Raleigh had such numerous and such white sepals that they looked like bloodroot.

There are two species of yellow violets on Rocky Knob, the round-leaved and the halberd-leaved. *Viola rotundifolia* blooms the first of April, and its earliness led Mrs. Dana to believe this is the species Bryant had in mind when he wrote—

> When beechen buds begin to swell,
> And woods the blue-birds warble know,
> The yellow violet's modest bell
> Peeps from the last year's leaves below.

To call this flower a bell carries poetic license too far, even though to some people bell and blossom are synonymous. The halberd-leaved violet (*V. hastata*), a southern species belonging to the section called mock pansies, occurs in mixed woods from Pennsylvania to Florida and Alabama, and is available from We-Du Nurseries. When the long, tapered, spear-shaped leaves are variegated, as they often are, with patches of gray-green or reddish bronze, they are more decorative than the small yellow flowers.

Rosa also lists the white Canada violet (*V. canadensis*), another of the mock pansies. In North Carolina it is found only in a few mountain counties where it blooms from

April to July. The buds are vinaceous, and there is a touch of yellow in the throats of the creamy flowers. Another mountain species, *V. striata*, has seeded itself all over my garden in Charlotte after I brought it from Raleigh, for sentimental reasons, leaving more valuable plants behind. It came from the cemetery in Marietta where several generations of our family are buried. Planting violets on graves is an ancient custom, but I have wondered how this species got there, as it is rare in Georgia, where it reaches its southern limit. When it blooms in mid-March or shortly thereafter, the clumps are tidy and covered with creamy flowers with violet stripes, but then it produces long and straggly stems which cover the basal leaves. Keeping them cut back is a terrible chore.

There is a tall, blue iris in the meadow below Rosa's house. Not knowing its Latin name, she calls it the orchid iris. When she sent it to me in bloom, it proved to be Iris *virginica*, the southern form of I. *versicolor*, a species ranging from Canada to Louisiana and Florida. As the specific name implies, it is variable as to color. The poorest forms, Dykes in *The Genus Iris* says, are small and pale, but the best have "large flowers of a good, deep blue-purple color, or even a velvety red-purple that borders on crimson." When Thoreau walked to White's Pond in June, 1853, he wrote in his Journal that blue flags were "growing thinly in the water about the shore," but when he went to Lupine Hill via Depot Field Brook in June of 1857, he described those he saw blooming in the meadows as having "variously streaked and colored petals." Another June day, he wrote that "some blue flags are quite a red purple, dark wine color." (The flags that I knew as a child were as blue as the waters of White's Pond. They grew in the ditches where the country road went through a shallow creek just beyond the last houses of Garysburg, North Carolina, the village we lived in when I was nine. I saw them there when I was riding my pony, one morning in May, and it was wonderful to me because they were the first wildflower I had found by myself and recognized by the picture in my flower book. Some sixty Mays later, when I drove over the same road, I found the creek running under it in a culvert—but the blue flags were still blooming.)

*

All along Route 3, there are other mountain folk selling flowers by mail and advertising in the *Review*, like Rosa Hicks.

Clara Trivette grows herbs like catnip and garlic and peppermint and garden flowers like candytuft and poppies and flame lily. When I ordered candytuft and poppies, she wrote, "I am mailing your plants today. I hope they live." They did. The petals of Mrs. Trivette's poppies are fiery red—"all silk and flame" as Ruskin said of the corn poppy when he saw it one Whitsunday. He might have added ashes, for the color of the ring of dark grey-violet stamens and the velvet embroidery on the ovary are like the flame burnt out. This glow has been seen as a real flame by several observers, including Goethe. The daughter of Linnaeus reported flashes of fire from scarlet nasturtiums on a sultry night, and others have seen flashes from lilies of the same color.

I was sure that Mrs. Trivette's flame lily would be *Lilium superbum*, but I have learned never to take anything for granted when identifying plants by their local names. I sent her a picture out of a catalog. "The picture you sent is a wild lily," she wrote. "I call it the tiger lily. The flame lily is different. It just blooms almost to the top of the stalk." She enclosed a colored photograph of a plant with upfacing orange flowers—almost surely one of the modern Rainbow Hybrids.

Mrs. Carl Presnell advertises "grass lilies." I wrote her to ask whether her grass lilies have clusters of six-petalled, white flowers and very narrow leaves with white stripes down the center. "I received your note about the grass lilies," she replied, "and they are like that." So now I know that they are the star of Bethlehem (*Ornithogalum umbellatum*), cherished in English gardens in the sixteenth century and cherished still in our mountains. *O. umbellatum* is a Mediterranean species that has become naturalized in this country. In gardens it should never be allowed to get a foothold, in spite of the purity and delicacy of the flowers when they blossom in April, opening only in full sun, a trait which gives them one of their common names, eleven-o'clock lady. This bulbous plant is unquestionably beautiful, but it is also a ruthless spreader.

*

The most interesting plants advertised in the *Review* come from the mountains and eastern Carolina, for the flowers of the piedmont are perennials, such as peonies, hostas, and named varieties of irises and daylilies.

Miss Bessie Bloodworth, my best correspondent in East Carolina, lives in Currie, a small community in Pender County. Our correspondence began with the Baptist plant, her name for *Alternanthera ficoidea* 'Bettzickiana,' usually known as Joseph's coat, a variegated foliage plant with leaves in tones of creamy yellow to salmon and bright red. "I think," Miss Bessie wrote, "that the Baptist plant got its name from changing color; you know the more sun it gets the more colors will be in it." She sent instructions with it. The instructions were, "Grow it like any other plant." With it came a free cutting of Jesstissue, as it is spelled in the market bulletin—now *Justicia carnea* (formerly given in *Hortus Third* as *Jacobinia carnea*), a member of the acanthus family and native to Brazil. It is hardy in New Orleans and will winter outside in northern Louisiana, though it takes a long time to recover there in spring. The spikes of curved, tubular flowers give it the name Brazilian-plume.

The usual market bulletin favorites are on Miss Bessie's list of pot plants: the spotted, or pink polka-dot plant (*Hypoestes phyllostachya*); the spider plant, several species and varieties of *Chlorophytum*, with white- or yellow-striped leaves and small, white flowers on slender stems that bend down under the weight of the flowers until the stems touch the soil and form new plants; widow's-tears or *Achimenes* in various colors but mostly the mournful purple; and the rubber plant (*Ficus elastica*), an evergreen fig with dark, glossy leaves up to eighteen inches long.

In India, *Ficus elastica* is an enormous tree. It became known as a source of rubber in 1810 when honey was sent in a wicker bottle from the mountains north of Silket to Dr. William Roxburgh, a Scot then in charge of the Calcutta Botanical Garden. The bottle was lined with resin from a tree that grew where the honey came from. When Dr. Roxburgh discovered that the resin was caoutchouc, the principal ingredient of Indian rubber, he imported young trees for the garden, where they grew luxuriantly. Soon afterwards this *Ficus* was introduced to England as a houseplant, capable of reaching sixteen feet in height in a tub, although in India and in southern Florida it grows to a height of a hundred feet with an equal spread. Enduring and long-lasting, rubber plants as houseplants sometimes become household pets. E. B. White had one called Hattie. When he left his apartment in New York to drive to his farm in Maine, Hattie went with him along with his son, a canary, and Freddie the dachshund.

I was most eager to see the plant Miss Bessie advertised as elephant tears, and disappointed to discover that it was a misprint for elephant-ears. Her gizzard cuttings are of *Iresine herbstii* 'aureo-reticulata,' commonly called chicken-gizzard plant for the network of fine yellow veins on the large, round leaves, which are notched at the apex.

Miss Bessie's amaryllis (*Hippeastrum*) is the gem of her collection, the most beautiful amaryllis I have ever seen, and far lovelier than the garish, thick-petaled hybrids of commerce. The flowers are large, to six inches across, with a six-pointed, yellow-green star in the center. The petals are fine in texture, but delicate and durable in substance. Their color is Ridgway's Apricot Orange, but Miss Bessie calls it salmon. I thought the bulb might winter outside in Currie, but she wrote me that "My amaryllis is a house plant if you want it to bloom in winter. For me it will bloom at Christmas and again in summer, but the bulb has to be large before it blooms at all." The bulb she sent me seemed small in comparison with those of other amaryllis, but it bloomed on the twentieth of March, with no repeat bloom later.

Miss Bessie's yard flowers have old-timey names. "Hummingbirds love the hummingbird plant," she wrote.

"They like to sit on it. I guess that's where it got its name. It has a lavender pink fuzzy bloom. The head of the bloom has a sweet odor. I have only a few left." Unfortunately, the plant she sent me was leafless when it came, and it perished before spring. When I asked for another, Miss Bessie wrote, "I lost all mine, and I don't know where you can find them." I think the plant must have been the old favorite spirea, Anthony Waterer (*Spirea × bumalda*), seldom seen nowadays except in the dooryards of country gardens.

The next time I ordered something from her, Miss Bessie replied, "I received your check, and I have what you want, but I am sick and I don't know when I will be able to fill it, if ever. I may have to have an operation on my head. So I am sending your check back. I thought it best. Remember me in prayer." Several weeks later she wrote that she was better. "I think I can get your plants now. I will try if you still want them. I am seventy-seven and I am thankful the good Lord let me live to wait on my father and my mother and my sister in their last days." She sent turkey-gobbler beads, wedding bells, carnation rose, and "the bush that stays green all winter." In the carton they came in, there still lingered the aroma of its original contents—"12 large-size foil pouches of flavor-fresh Red Man tobacco, America's best chew." And there were instructions. "The reason I ask you to water them good, I was afraid to put anything damp around them, and I would mulch them too. The wedding bells bloom early, and make a large bush. I don't know where their name came from. You know flowers has a lot of names. The flowers of wedding bells are a gold color. I believe you asked about the size of the green bush. It will grow tall, but I keep mine cut back. I do not know the name. It came from an old English estate. It stays green all winter, and in spring has heads of green bloom. You asked where the turkey gobbler beads came from. They belonged to my grandmother who was a great flower lover. If she had of lived, she would now be one hundred and seventy-five years [in 1975]. Anytime you want to know anything that I can help you with, I will."

The turkey-gobbler beads were in fruit when they came, so I was able to identify the plant at once as the coral berry, or Indian currant (*Symphoricarpos orbiculatus*), which is also called turkeyberry, the berries being the color of a turkey's wattles. Wedding bells is *Forsythia viridissima*. It blooms in February and sometimes repeats in the fall. The carnation rose is a bramble, *Rubus coronarius*, a different species than the one I saw blooming at Rosa Hicks's place. Widely grown in the South, it is hardy as far north as New Jersey. In the late nineteenth century it was sold by Bobbink & Atkins as the brier rose, but I think the market bulletins are the only source for it now. I first saw it in Shreveport, Louisiana. "The bush that stays green all winter" is *Euonymus fortunei*, a shrub spread freely by the birds.

"Speaking of old flowers," Miss Bessie wrote, "I have the old timey bridal wreath spiraea, you know it blooms real early, and I have the Christmas honeysuckle. It grows in a large stiff bush and blooms at Christmas. I know it has the sweetest odor of any plant I ever did see. I have the blooming almond and the sweet shrub." The double pink form of the almond is the variety usually found in southern gardens, but it is hardy in New England. Mrs. Earle says it was, after the lilac, the favorite shrub of her childhood. She also cherished the sweet shrub (*Calycanthus floridus*), for the scent of the dark red flowers, "an aromatic fragrance somewhat like the ripest Pineapples of the tropics, but still richer." The leaves and bark are spicy. I suppose the name Carolina allspice was given to it by Mark Catesby in 1726 when he found it near Charleston and sent it to England.

I thought Miss Bessie's "blue boxwood vine evergreen" would be *Vinca minor* and creeping charlie would be *Nepeta hederacea* (which is now *Glechoma hederacea*), but I sent specimens of each to make sure. "The pieces you sent," she wrote, "are what I have advertised."

Miss Bessie had promised to send me the names of "any new kind of old-fashion flowers," but the last time I heard from her, she said, "I am not growing as many flowers as I used to, for my health is not so good. I hope you feel real good. Love always, Bessie Bloodworth."

*

Names of three interesting plants—a vine, a shrub, and a tree, all from gardens on the coastal plain—have appeared in the *Review*. I sent Miss Marie Lewis a leaf of *Akebia quinata*, asking her to compare it with her chocolate vine. "Yes," she said, "the leaf appears to be exactly like those of the old Southern chocolate vine. Mine has been here in Mount Olive nearly a hundred year, and I have never heard it called anything else. Your description of the flower fits. They are chocolate or deep purple, and have a spicy odor. Thanks for giving me the correct name." I had never heard a common name for this plant, but I now find this one in *Hortus Third*. In *The Fragrant Path*, Louise Beebe Wilder called it raisin vine, another name I never heard elsewhere, but some say the flowers smell like grapes. She says, "It gives to the night a spicy fragrance that it quite withholds from the day." Perhaps this absence of scent during the day holds true in the North, but after we moved to Raleigh when I was a child, I knew its fragrance intimately from the bower covering the summerhouse. In April, the maroon-purple flowers, male and female, hang in clusters among the five-fingered leaves. The female flowers have three cupped petals, with dark drops of nectar at the tips of the pistils. The large Tyrian purple fruits are about the size and shape of pawpaws, and they are edible, although *Hortus Third* calls them "insipid." Akebia is hardy to Zone 5. It is deciduous in the North, semievergreen in the Middle South, and evergreen in the Deep South. It will grow in sun or shade and can be used as a ground cover, but it must be kept under control or it will smother other plants.

Mrs. Charles Corbett, who lives in Ivanhoe, a community in Sampson County, advertises the oak-leaved hydrangea, which William Bartram discovered in southern Georgia near the main branch of the Altamaha River and described in *Travels in the Carolinas, Georgia, and Florida* (1773–1778). "I observed here," he wrote, "a very singular and beautiful shrub, which I suppose is a species of Hydrangea. It grows coppices and clumps near or on the banks of rivers and creeks; many stems usually rise from the root spreading itself greatly on all sides by suckers and offsets; the stems grow five or six feet high. . . . The panicles are truly permanent, remaining on the plant until they dry or decay." He saw them the first week in July, when the white, sterile flowers were turning to warm tones of rose and fawn. As they grow older, the tones deepen to russet and wine. In Charlotte they come into bloom at the end of May, but they blossom earlier in the Deep South. Caroline Dorman wrote me one May that they had been blooming for weeks at Briarwood. "Lovely," she said, "I can smell them from my bedroom window." The panicles are a foot long, and the large leaves are shaped like those of the red oak. Although it is a southern species, ranging from mid-Georgia to Florida and Mississippi, it is grown as far north as Zone 5, and will come back from the roots if the tops are killed to the ground.

When I saw Mrs. John Gore's advertisement of seeds of the goldenrain tree from Monticello, I wrote to ask her about it. I knew that Thomas Jefferson planted there *Koelreuteria paniculata* (introduced from China into England in 1763), and that it had been planted in his restored garden, but I wondered how it got to Mrs. Gore in Rockingham. She answered that she had read about it in *A Southern Garden*, and that she and her husband had bought a tree at the gift shop at Monticello. She said she sold seed because the volunteer plants are not easy to transplant. This native of China and Korea seeds very freely, and has escaped in Orange County. I have seen it in full bloom in Chapel Hill in early June. The large panicles of small, pale yellow flowers stand above the finely textured foliage to make a quite becoming sight.

*

In the "Seeds and Plants for Sale" columns of the *Review*, I find dried hops and "Hops (alive) plants and instructions to make yeast from only hops and boiled potatoes." Some local delicacies include creasy, candy roaster (or rooster) seed, and old-timey grass nuts. Creasy is winter cress (*Barbarea vulgaris*), a European member of the mustard family that has become naturalized in this country, and is grown or gathered by country people as a potherb. It is a perennial, but seed I got from my friends in Banner Elk and sowed in late summer came up and bloomed in the spring. When I sowed more in hot rainy weather in early summer, they sprouted almost overnight. The young leaves are as delicate and piquant as watercress, and I like them even when they get older and tougher and sufficiently more piquant to be called bitter cress, although that name seems somewhat harsh to me. Creasy is an herb of the third-century saint, Saint Barbara, and it is green on her Feast Day, the fourth of December. She is a popular saint, often seen in paintings carrying a miniature of the tower in which her father shut her up out of jealousy of her lovers. When he discovered that she had secretly become a Christian, he lovingly beheaded her, whereupon he was struck by a bolt of lightning. Saint Barbara is turned to for protection during thunderstorms.

From the descriptions I gather that candy roasters are various kinds of pumpkins or melons raised for their seeds, edible when roasted: "Seeds of sixty-five pound melon when roasted they taste like a sweet potato." The old-timey grass nuts in the *Review* are *Cyperus esculentus sativus*, the yellow nut sedge of the Mississippi *Bulletin*, an edible sedge that has naturalized in the Southeast. I got some from Mrs. Sam Echerd, who wrote, "You pick them up out of the bunch when you take them up before frost, wash them, and then they are ready to eat. Let them dry before putting them away." The tubers are also called chufas or earth nuts, and they taste pleasantly of almonds mixed with raisins. Pigs and chickens relish them, as do people, who can grind them and mix them with flour to make bread and cookies. But I have no intention of letting them in my garden, where they might be as hard to get rid of as their relative, *C. rotundus*, the dreaded purple nut sedge or nut grass, referred to by weed scientists as the worst weed in the world.

I wrote Miss Bessie Baker to inquire about her marsh clematis (*Clematis crispa*), a fragile vine that grows in low, wet places along the coastal plain from Virginia to Florida and along the Gulf Coast to Texas. It is a plant I remember fondly. When we lived in Raleigh, it was given to me by Miss Rosa Hill, an old lady who used to work with me on the Altar Guild at Christ Church. When I picked her up to go to the parish house, I would stop to admire the flowers in her dooryard garden, especially this clematis, which she called bluebell and cherished because it had come from her grandmother's garden and because the fragrant, pale blue, urn-shaped flowers bloomed from mid-April well into summer. I left Miss Rosa's clematis behind in Raleigh when I moved to Charlotte, in the mistaken notion that I could replace it easily. (It is now available from Woodlanders.)

Miss Bessie Baker's advertisement in the *Review* gave me hope for having this beloved clematis, so rich in good memories, once again. But my letter to her was returned unopened, with "Deceased" stamped across the address.

The Other Market Bulletins

Caroline Dorman introduced me to the *Louisiana Weekly Farm Bulletin*, which has not existed since 1966—a great pity, for it had its own special character. You had only to open it to see the French imprint on the fixed pattern of the Deep South, in the taste, the customs, and especially the names: LeBeau, LaFleur, Thibodeux, Dieudonne, Arcineaux.

Alcide Arcineaux had for sale a black mare "good for a lady to ride, good for barrel racing and Parade." There were frequent notices of horse shows in the Louisiana bulletins: "quarter horses, parade, barrel racing, roping, cutting, etc. will be shown." There were reminders about annual strawberry festivals, the Marydale Farms Angus bull and female sale at St. Francisville with Angus barbecue served starting at 11:30 a.m., rodeo performances at 8:00 p.m. in Lake Charles.

There were a great many more vegetables, in far greater variety, in the Louisiana bulletin than in the bulletins of the other southern states. Collards and cowpeas were common, but there were also velvet beans, bur artichokes, Chinese cabbages, Creole leeks, cushaws, and mirlitons. Cushaws are crookneck winter squashes. Mirlitons (*Sechium edule*) are something like summer squashes, but of a more delicate flavor; their tubers, as well as their fruits, may be cooked in various ways. There were also ground artichokes, a common local name for another tuber, the Jerusalem artichoke.

I must digress briefly about the Jerusalem artichoke (*Helianthus tuberosus*), one of the most constant offerings in all of the market bulletins, which can be tasty, even though gardeners must keep a wary eye on it for its invasive ways. I have always thought of the Jerusalem artichoke as southern, but on looking it up I find that its range is from Georgia to Canada. It was a traditional food of many Indian tribes, and was already in cultivation on Cape Cod when Champlain went there in 1604 in search of a site for a new settlement. By 1622 it was being hawked in the streets of London. Tobias Venner described it in *Via Recta* as a "roote usually eaten with butter, vinegar, and pepper." English gardeners soon learned that in the ground the tubers bear watching, and explained the name as meaning horti- or hartichoke, because the plant chokes the garden, or the heart. One fanciful seventeenth-century writer observed that Error is like the Jerusalem artichoke: "Plant it where you will, it over-runnes the Garden and chokes the Heart."

Jerusalem artichokes were relished by the Victorians. Mrs. Earle, who liked to introduce recipes in her books, said they could be made into a soup, which was called Palestine soup, since some people wrongly thought they were native to Jerusalem because the name misled them.

She also thought them tasty if pureed like turnips or fried in thin slices like potato chips. The only way they were not good, she said, was the usual way, plain, boiled with a sauce of flour and butter. The best way, however, was au gratin, especially "using half Parmesan and half Gruyère and a very small piece of shallot."

Mrs. Earle believed that the artichoke was much better if planted from fresh seed rather than from old tubers. But it is usually the tubers that the market bulletin women offer, generally in December: "Jerusalem artichokes; will make good crisp pickles; washed & sacked." It is as pickles that I use them, and, following Mrs. Earle's precedent, I offer the following recipe, from South Carolina. Wash and scrub well one peck of artichokes. Drop in a weak salt-water solution (½ cup salt to 1 gallon water) for two hours. Make a spice vinegar composed of: 2½ to 5 cups sugar (depending on preference); 5 cups vinegar; 2 tablespoons each of celery seed, white mustard seed, black mustard seed, and whole allspice; 1 stick cinnamon; 1 tablespoon whole cloves; 1 medium-sized onion, sliced; 1 garlic clove; several small red-hot peppers; ½ cup olive oil. Heat spice vinegar to boiling to melt sugar. Set aside. Fill sterilized jars with artichokes. Cover with vinegar to very brim. Seal and store in refrigerator until ready to use, but allow to steep for at least a week.

The plant that was advertised in the Louisiana bulletins as crybaby is *Erythrina crista-galli*, the Brazilian coral tree. It is considered to be hardy as far north as the District of Columbia. Beyond that, the roots are taken up and stored in a dry place (some say a moist place) until spring. In my garden it is killed to the ground by the first hard frost. New shoots come up in May and quickly make a large bush about five feet tall and nearly twice as wide. The flowers are like enormous nopal-red sweet peas in spikes up to a yard long. There is a burst of bloom in July, or sometimes in June, and then a few spikes all through summer and fall. All during the season the large, three-parted, gray-green leaves look as if the dew is still on them, even on the hottest and driest days.

Cashmere bouquet is the Louisiana name for *Clerodendrum fragrans*, now called *C. philippinum*. I first saw it in Shreveport gardens, where it is a great favorite in spite of its weedy appearance and invasive habit. To me the charming little bunches of pink-tinted, double, intensely fragrant flowers do not make it worthy of space in the garden, and I cannot imagine taking the trouble to grow it indoors. *Clerodendrum bungei* came to me from Louisiana as the Mexican hydrangea, though it is native to China, and I think it is what the farm women call Mexicali rose. I have been trying to get rid of it for over twelve years, and have given lots away to gardeners who refused to heed my warning when they saw the large heads of wine-red buds and laelia-pink flowers in midsummer and fall. The leaves, like those of Cashmere bouquet, are fetid when crushed. Another clerodendrum grown in Louisiana, the bowing-lady (*C. indicum*), is as invasive as the rest, and its unattractive tubular flowers are open only a short while in the morning. I have never given it a trial, and I don't know whether it would be hardy in the North Carolina piedmont.

Another shrub that was in the bulletin is the Easter rose (*Rubus coronarius*), Miss Bessie Bloodworth's carnation rose. I found out that it is almost as common in North Carolina as in Louisiana, but here it blooms later and is sometimes called Mother's Day rose. It appears in all the southern market bulletins under various names, including blackberry rose and bridal rose. In New Orleans they call it nun's rose, because of legends that it came from France with the Casquette Brides that nuns brought over to marry Frenchmen living in Louisiana. I have heard that it is root hardy in New York. The Easter rose is invasive, but I have never found it impossible to control, though it is difficult to keep it in order, as the prickles are numerous and unpleasantly sharp. The old canes should be removed after blooming, and the new ones trained to some support; otherwise, they lie on the ground and take root at every joint. They grow to eight or ten feet in a season, and are well furnished with bright leaves and large, double, pure white flowers.

In Louisiana, the roses in country gardens are much the same as those in Mississippi: the Florida red rose, the Florida white rose, the Seven Sisters, Maréchal Niel, Louis Philippe. In New Orleans a small polyantha called Picayune goes from garden to garden. One went to Birmingham and then to Ohio, where it seems to be hardy. It grows three feet high. Cuttings begin to bloom as soon as they take root, and they bloom steadily all through the growing season. The flowers are something like that of The Fairy, but smaller, daintier, and more delicately tinted.

It is well to remember that in Louisiana lady slippers will be balsam (*Impatiens balsamina*), snowdrops will be snowflakes (*Leucojum aestivum*), and bachelor's buttons will be gomphrena, the globe amaranth. Some of the fanciful names of the countryside are: lady's-bouquet (Cashmere bouquet?); flaming fountain or sea willow (*Amaranthus tricolor salicifolius*); Creole box (*Buxus microphylla* japonica), a good shrub for climates too hot for English box; and splendiferous red sage (I have no idea).

The Louisiana bulletins advertised a wealth of vines: coral vine (*Antigonon leptopus*), sometimes listed as rosa de montana; passion vine (mostly the exotic tropical species); yellow bignonia (which I take to be *Macfadyena unquiscati*); and the firecracker vine and the potato vine. The firecracker vine (*Manettia inflata*) grows out-of-doors in Shreveport, but I lost it the first winter here. As a houseplant it blooms freely and over a long period, either in a pot or a hanging basket in a sunny window. The flowers are slender, scarlet tubes with bright yellow tips. The potato vine of the market bulletins is not *Solanum jasminoides*, although that is also grown in Gulf Coast gardens. It is *Dioscorea bulbifera*, the air potato, a tropical vine that can be grown as an annual. I once planted the tubers in May, and the slender vines shot up to ten feet, even producing small potatoes before frost caught them. The long-stemmed, heart-shaped leaves have a coppery luster. I see no mention of it in books on indoor gardening, but I should think it would be a decorative window vine, planted outside in a pot and then taken inside in the fall. It grows in sun or shade.

I wrote one of the regular advertisers in the Louisiana bulletin, Mrs. R. M. Snider of Lake Charles, to ask about some of the interesting vines she listed. She said that ram's-horn is a species of *Vigna* with spiral buds. The flowers are pink and ivory and very fragrant. Another vigna, *V. caracalla*, the snail flower or corkscrew, is a perennial that can be grown in the garden as an annual. It was once in favor as a houseplant. Mrs. Snider lists the cruel vine (*Araujia sericifera*) under its old name, *Physianthus*. It is said to bloom the first year from seed, but I find that it takes two. Although it comes from southern Brazil it is hardy in North Carolina. It seeds itself freely, but it is not evergreen, as it is in warmer climates. In the garden, the very white, very fragrant flowers, sometimes giving it the name poor-man's stephanotis, begin to open in June. They are still in bloom in early fall when the large, decorative, apple green fruits mature. The vine is called cruel because moths visiting the flowers jam their probosces in slits in the anthers and become temporarily entangled. They emerge covered with pollen, thus insuring cross-pollination. Seeds are available from Thompson and Morgan. And Mrs. Snider has high regard for the cassabanana vine (*Sicana odorifera*), of whose fruit she makes delicious preserves. It looks like a big cucumber, and when it is ripe it is the color of an orange and smells like a banana. It is another tropical perennial that can be grown in cooler regions as an annual.

Trees in the Louisiana bulletin were mostly advertised under their common names, some of them local. Fishbait trees are catalpas, raised for the crops of worms that feed on their leaves. Rain trees are not the tropical *Samanea saman*, but *Melia azedarach umbraculiformis*, a form of chinaberry. Leverwood is *Ostrya virginiana*, the hop hornbam. Bois d'arc is *Maclura pomifera*, commonly called Osage orange except in the French country and in Texas and Arkansas (where bois d'arc is pronounced "Boh dark," with either syllable being accented, depending on the speaker). The Indians made their bows from its wood. Nowadays, it is used mostly for fence posts.

I had come to depend on the Louisiana bulletin for the pictures it called up of a part of the South that is kin to,

but still different from, the place where I live. I miss
it—but I suppose there may come a time when there
aren't any market bulletins being published at all.

*

The *South Carolina Market Bulletin* is rich in old-time flowers
and old-time names. Clematis is porch vine, and the
snowberry (*Symphoricarpos albus*) is ice-apple. Coral bush
(*S. orbiculatus*) sometimes is listed as red snowberry, but
also as birds-eye.

Some of the names go back to the eighteenth century.
In our mountains, kalmia is still called ivy, as it was in the
letters between Collinson and Custis. "There's two or
three plants in your country I should be glad of,"
Collinson wrote, "viz. the Dogwood Tree and a sort of
Laurell or Bay . . . by some improperly called Ivy and if
the sheep Eat it Kills them." Later he wrote, "The sorrel
Trees thrive well as pretty Curiosities, but the greatest is
the Beautifull plant call'd an Ivy which you formerly sent
Mee." The South Carolina bulletin sometimes lists mountain ivy, as well as mountain pink (*Phlox subulata*), mountain buddie (*Buddleia?*), mountain hydrangea, and mountain holly.

One of the regular advertisers in this bulletin is Ethel
Harmon, who lives in Saluda. The bulletin isn't mailed to
anyone who lives outside of the state, but Mrs. Harmon
will send her list of bulbs, old-fashioned flowers, and
wildflowers to anyone who asks for it. I got in touch with
her, many years ago, through Caroline Dorman and her
sister-in-law, Ruth Dorman. "Mrs. Dorman and I were
great Pen Pals for many years," she wrote me in May,
1962,

and I learned to love her. Ruth passed on, and Caroline Dorman wrote me of her death. Since then, she and I have corresponded quite a lot. Miss Caroline must be a wonderful person. Wish I knew her personally. She can give you so much on flowers, on the names and on growing them. I wish she could see our wild flowers in the early spring. Our woods have so many pretty things that most people pass unnoticed.

I asked Mrs. Harmon about the same time if she recalled any common names that might be local to South Carolina, and she wrote back to say that she had been trying to think up some names for me.

Did you know that the dogtooth violet is called wild peanut? The bulbs are edible and have a taste of green peanuts. Bluets are forget-me-nots. Hepatica is cat's paw. We used to have a shrub, now called butterfly bush, only our blooms were smaller. If anyone asked the name, we'd say kiss-me-and-I'll-tell-you. Irises are called Easter lilies, and so are Atamasco lilies. Atamasco lilies are also called naked ladies. I have sold thousands of grape hyacinths as blue bottles or blue jugs to customers who asked for them by those names.

I have never before heard that the bulbs of the dogtooth violet are edible, but Mrs. Grieve, in *A Modern Herbal*, says they are emetic and Mrs. Lounsberry, in *Southern Wild Flowers and Trees*, reports that the mountain people collected the plants before they flowered, for medicinal purposes. Naked ladies for atamasco lilies is a good example of a transferred common name. In England, it refers to the meadow saffron. As for kiss-me-and-I'll-tell-you, my friend Mr. W. O. Freeland of Columbia, South Carolina, sent me the old butterfly bush. Its narrow spikes of flowers are not as handsome as those of the modern hybrids. The butterflies, however, prefer the old ones.

*

The Georgia *Farmers Market Bulletin* comes out weekly, "address requests to be added to or removed from the mailing list, to circulation manager, Market Bulletin, Atlanta." I asked to have my name put on the mailing list while I was in search of a certain scarlet amaryllis (probably a garden form of *Hippeastrum striatum*), and I became so attached to the employment columns that I have never had it removed. A refined lady is wanted "to do gardening on a Christian farm—should love flowers." A sixty-five-year-old man, "alone, slightly handicapped, wants job mending fences for room, board, laundry, and smoking tobacco; will go anywhere, but prefers small family or elderly couple and will need bus fare." One man wants to catch, load, and haul wild cattle. Another man wants to shoe horses—"hot, corrective shoeing." A man "aged fifty-nine, abstainer and vegetarian, needs work badly on a farm; has well-indexed books, catalogs, encyclopedias, maps, etc. for colleges and public libraries—will work part time free, preferably with humanitarians."

The roses in the Georgia bulletins are mostly climbing ones, the Cherokee, the Banksia, Maréchal Niel, and some pretty ones, such as Mary Wallace and Dr. Van Fleet, which are no longer in fashion and not often found in the trade. One advertiser offers rose cuttings for free. Another will send seeds of snow-on-the-mountain to anyone who asks and sends a self-addressed, stamped envelope.

In the flower columns I find kiss-me-I-tell-you (which may be the old buddleia, but just as easily may not), weeping Mary, butterfly lilies. And the umbrella bush—I hope anyone who knows what that is will let me know too. There is a good bit of colorful spelling: holly hawk, sherry poppy, rose of Charon, and Chaster daisy.

In the miscellaneous columns pecans can be found, also bamboo canes for knocking them down from the trees; mountain-wildflower and sourwood honey "as the bees make it"; country-cured ham and sausage; bird-house gourds, king cobra snake gourds, African monster ("world's largest gourd"), Hercules'-club and milk-bottle gourds; Georgia cane syrup; and, of course, the beer seed, which becomes ever more mysterious to me the more explanations I hear.

The special handicraft columns seem to be peculiar to the Georgia bulletins. They offer children's clothes, handpainted pillowcases, band or bib aprons, and old-fashioned sunbonnets: ruffled bonnets, button or crown bonnets with long or short tails. And quilts: Fallen Leaves, Family Circle, Endless Stairs, Step-around-the-Mountain, and Grandmother's Flower Garden. "Mama's rich in quilts," Virgie Rainey said, when Miss Katie died. (We are back where we began, with *The Golden Apples*.) "Double Muscadine Hulls," Virgie said, "Road to Dublin, Starry Sky, Strange Spider Web, Hands All Round, Double Wedding Ring." The farm women sell patterns as well as quilts: "116-year-old quilt pattern, Rocky Road to California. Dove in the Window, over a hundred years old." And tatting. Tatting seems to be a Georgia specialty. It is often advertised as "small." We used to get the most minute and fine tatting from an old lady in Americus.

I like the horse, mule, and pony columns in this bulletin: "pleasure horse with stocking feet, gelding, nice manners, good gaits"; "gray jenny, gentle with children": and a "child-broke poney." And I am, for the moment anyway, reassured to find in the farm equipment column of the Georgia bulletin advertisements for a one-horse wagon and breecher, a mule-drawn mowing machine, and a blacksmith's anvil with blower, visor, hammer, and the proverbial tongs.

*

The Alabama *Farmers' For Sale, Want, and Exchange Bulletin* is published twice a month by the Department of Agriculture and Industries in Montgomery. "Items can be accepted from farmers only," the departmental commissioner says, "and the materials must be farm products, implements, and articles used in the furtherance of agricultural industry." No items of city property can be accepted, he says, and no typewriters, canaries, guns, or dogs. (The Mississippi and the North Carolina bulletins are the only ones in which I have seen dogs listed, and some of the Mississippi flower growers have told me they resent the space given to dogs, their qualities and their pedigrees, while the flower lists are trimmed).

Rare wildflowers are sometimes listed in the Alabama bulletin, also the curious feather hyacinth (*Muscari comosum plumosum*) so treasured in old gardens all over the South, and a great variety of Roman hyacinths. In spring and fall bulbs of "old fashioned, single, sweet-scented early hyacinths, blue, pink, and white" are offered. Sometimes the farm women call them French hyacinths, and they are right, because they originally came from France. They are not very hardy, so I do not know how far north they will grow, but I have heard of some in Pennsylvania.

Mrs. Brakefield, who writes me about the old bulbs she collects for her garden in Birmingham, says the hyacinths are her favorites. "I have four shades of blue," she says, "and hundreds of them. Our last winters have been too cold for the white ones, but I have a beautiful double pink that I ordered through the Alabama bulletin and also found for sale by some mountain women in Tennessee. I also have a double blue hyacinth."

Sometimes dewdrop bulbs are advertised. A nurseryman told me a customer once asked him if he had any dewdrops, and he found out that it was *Leucojum aestivum* that she wanted.

Collections of yard plants, "assorted kinds," are offered in the flower columns of the Alabama bulletin, and seed by the thimbleful—sultana, marble vine, poppies from France. Wild petunias will be *Ruellia ciliosa*, a pretty, blue-violet flower that is native from New Jersey to Florida and Texas. I rather think that the "yellow rose-shaped plant, spring-flowering (name unknown)" will turn out to be the double (and prevailing) form of *Kerria japonica*. Other local names of interest are: Dutchman's-bearded-pipe, cardinal betony fern, the bursting cardinal heart shrub, yellow buttons, nodding toad (a trillium), and Vinca Manor. *Euonymus americana*, the American spindle tree, is generally known as bursting-heart, and in the market bulletins it is often called heart-bursting-with-love. The cardinal heart must come somehow from the French name for the European spindle-tree. They call it *Bonnet de prêtre*, because the capsules are something like a three-cornered hat. The usual names for the American spindle-tree that I am used to are strawberry bush and wahoo, wahoo being the Indian name. Mrs. Lounsberry says it is also called burning bush.

I sometimes see peacock fern advertised. It is *Selaginella uncinata*, a mossy groundcover used to carpet shady parts of southern gardens, but probably not hardy much further north than North Carolina. Where the shade is deep enough, and the ground moist enough, it takes on the metallic shimmer of peacock feathers. It is also known as rainbow moss, and Eudora Welty says she has heard it called love-in-a-tangle, so it may be the love-tangle of the Mississippi bulletins.

Peacocks themselves are advertised frequently, and on occasion "real peacock tail feathers to four feet long." A male peacock is offered in exchange for Silver Spangle Hamburgs, and a pair of African owls in exchange for Golden Pheasant hens, or blooming-size amaryllis bulbs —"any color but red." Miss Donna Tidwell, a regular patron of the bulletin, will trade "a pair of common goats, Big Red peanuts, or pecans, for a hundred-pound hog. Bring your exchange, and get yours."

The Alabama vegetables are much the same as those of the other southern states—sweet potatoes, cowpeas, and old-fashioned blue collards—but the strawberry-flavored rhubarb seems to be a specialty. And, as in the other bulletins, Jerusalem artichokes for planting and pickling are in good supply.

*

The *Florida Market Bulletin* introduces another world. The columns for "Ornamental Plants, Seeds, and Plants from Farm and Grove" add the wealth of the tropics to the flowers and herbs of country gardens and the shrubs and trees of the Deep South. Mangoes and avocados and Sicilian lemons take the place of peaches and pears, and instead of blackberries, horse apples, and "big red June plums" there are pineapples, African gooseberries, eggfruits, and governor's plums.

The columns are full of the strange or beautiful names of tropical plants: the ear tree, the eggfruit, and the sausage tree; the raintree, the flame tree, and frangipani; mountain ebony; and golden dewdrop, golden shower, and golden rain. Mountain-ebony is the orchid tree (*Bauhinia variegata*). Golden dewdrop is *Duranta repens*, a small tree in the tropics, but a straggling and eventually doomed shrub in my garden in Raleigh, years ago. It lived for several years after I brought it up from St. Simon's Island, blooming fitfully, with lilac flowers followed by golden berries. Then I moved it and it died. The golden raintree of Florida gardens is not the well-known *Koelreuteria paniculata*, which is hardy to Boston, but the tenderer species, *K. bipinnata*. I gave it a trial in Charlotte, but it didn't survive. I was disappointed, for it is said to have peach-colored flowers in August and September that are followed by inflated fruits that look like the flower bracts of bougainvillea. I have heard that the young trees are somewhat frost tender but this tree proves hardy as far north as Silver Spring, Maryland.

The tropical raintree (*Samanea saman*) is a wide-spreading shade tree of the mimosa family. The leaves close at night and before showers, which may account for its name, although there's another possibility. It is said to be one of the trees attacked by cicadas that wound the branches. When juice drops from the wounds, the tree seems to produce a shower.

The ear tree is an enterolobium, another relative of the

mimosa, a quick-growing tree with pinnate leaves that make a light shade. For fifty cents, I think it would be fun to try an ear tree seedling in a pot on a patio. Some of these fine-leaved tropical trees take kindly to pots. "Of all my house plants," Ernesta Ballard writes in *Garden in Your House*, "the silk oak, *Grevillea robusta*, is almost the most satisfactory. It grows fast, and its fern-like foliage adds a graceful note to my window garden. If you want to raise a house plant from seed, this is the one to try. The seeds are large, they germinate quickly, and in one year the seedling may reach a height of three feet. . . . Here in the East, where they must spend the winter indoors, they never get too large for the house, and I doubt that they will ever flower. They like some sun each day." I feel sure that Mrs. Ballard's houseplant gives her as much pleasure as the sixty-foot silk oak in Dr. Nehrling's garden much further south gave him. "In March, when in flower," he says in *My Garden in Florida*, "it looks from the distance like a huge flame."

In my garden, I like to try tropical plants for a season, even though I know that they will not live through the winter. To take just one example, one year I planted a Mexican flame vine (*Senecio confusus*) which came from Florida in a small can. It was early May when I set it out, and it rapidly covered many feet of the garden wall. It bloomed gloriously from the eighth of September until the first of November, when our first hard frost put an end to its fiery daisy-like flowers and the plant itself.

Lots of bulbs appear in the columns of the Florida market bulletins: haemanthus, habranthus, amaryllis, lycoris, zephyranthes, and glory lilies. There are the old roses, hybrid hibiscus, yucca, and the usual plants of country gardens, the sunflowers, daturas, and all the rest.

The Florida bulletins are published twice every month by the Florida State Marketing Bureau in Jacksonville. The tropical plants are fascinating, and the bulletins are very businesslike. They are not nearly so folksy as the other market bulletins of the Gulf States, and this absence of the personal element makes them not quite as much fun to read and ponder.

The Herb Gatherers

The Healing Herbs

Sometimes, when I am reading the market bulletins, I have a feeling that herb lore is still as much a part of the lives of the country people as the stars or the seasons. And I am reminded of Mrs. Todd, in Sarah Orne Jewett's, *The Country of the Pointed Firs*, "an ardent lover of herbs, both wild and tame," and of her garden where the sea breezes were laden—

> not only with sweet-brier and sweet-Mary, but balm and sage and borage and mint, wormwood and southernwood. . . . At one side of this herb plot were other growths of a rustic pharmacopaeia, great treasures and rarities among the commoner herbs. There were some strange and potent odors that roused a dim sense and remembrance of something in the forgotten past. Some of these might once have belonged to sacred and mystic rites, and have had

some occult knowledge handed with them down
the centuries; but now they pertained only to hum-
ble compounds brewed at intervals with molasses
or vinegar or spirits in a small caldron on Mrs. Todd's
kitchen stove. They were dispensed to suffering
neighbors, who usually came at night, bringing their
own ancient-looking vials to be filled. . . . It may not
have been only the common ails of humanity with
which she tried to cope; it seemed sometimes as if
love and hate and jealousy and adverse winds at sea
might also find their proper remedies in Mrs. Todd's
garden.

Mrs. Todd's mother said, "The time o' sickness and failin'
has got to come. But Almiry's got an herb that's good for
everything."

There is an overtone of love and hate and jealousy in
the very names of the herbs listed. They make me think
of a recipe for a conjure-bag: "A pair of Adam-and-Eve-
roots; wahoo bark; devil's shoestring; asafetida—roots
must be dug when there is blood in the moon." Adam-
and-Eve root is an old name for the little white orchid
Aplectrum hyemale and wahoo is the southern elm, *Ulmus
alata*, also called witch elm. Mrs. Grieve's *Herbal* says that
asafetida has been in use as a medicine since the twelfth
century. Until a few years ago, it was still available in
drugstores that catered to country people. The Charlotte
Drug Company used to carry it, and people bought it.
When I asked a pharmacist there what they bought it for,
he said, "They wear it and eat it." Now this company is
no more, but some of my contemporaries remember
going to school with asafetida bags hung around their

necks to keep them from catching colds and children's diseases. Some say it must have worked as they were never sick. Our family maid thought asafetida was good for colic in babies, and that the gum steeped in whiskey would cure indigestion. Before the days of embalming, people wore asafetida bags to funerals.

One of the patrons of the *Mississippi Market Bulletin* has been Dr. R. L. Sanders. Said to be "the greatest living authority on botanical medicines," he advertises "herbs of all kinds." He says that when he was a little boy he followed his grandmother, the root-doctor, as she gathered roots, herbs, bark, leaves, berries, flowers, and pollen. All medicines, she said, come out of the earth. Every morning before breakfast, from April through August, she made her grandchildren drink a brew of the bark of sassafras and prickly ash to ward off fever and chills. She was celebrated for her rheumatism medicine made from five kinds of bark and two kinds of roots. When she extracted the teeth of her family, neighbors, and tenants, she first rubbed their gums with a dried leaf powder, so that there was no pain and very little bleeding. For brushing the teeth she recommended ground comfrey root. She kept all her teeth until she was eighty-eight. "She walked erect," Dr. Sanders says, "never had an ache or pain, and wasn't laid up with rheumatism like old lady Barlow, who refused to go in for Grandma's 'herb juice.' Grandma lived to be ninety-three, and when she died it was not from illness. She was just worn out, like an old wagon."

*

"Strong red sassafras roots" are advertised in the Georgia bulletin throughout the year. They are sold by the quart or half gallon, "freshly dug and water cleaned, cut into small pieces ready to boil into table-use tea." The bark from the roots is more expensive than the whole root. White sassafras roots are available too, but the red is always preferred. I asked Sadie Samuel, who grew up on a South Carolina farm and used to dig roots for her mother, what the difference between red and white is. She said, "One kind grows on one tree and the other grows on another," which turned out to be true, but nevertheless puzzled me, since there is only one American species, *Sassafras albidum*. After some inquiry, I finally solved the puzzle when I got the answer from James Long of the Georgia Department of Agriculture. In a letter, he wrote, "The root color may vary with age, size, and rate of growth. The old roots normally have a very thin, white layer of water-transporting wood just beneath the bark, and a larger nonconductive red area in the center. This corresponds to the heart wood (red) and the sap wood (white) of the stem."

Sadie says she still drinks sassafras tea in the spring, but makes it from chips from the supermarket. Rosa Hicks in North Carolina still digs the roots for tea and for flavoring candy, but she no longer uses sassafras and other plants in the ways her parents and grandparents did. "We don't use any plants for medicine ourselves," she says, "but they did when I was growing up. Maybe they had just as good medicine as we can buy, because they knew their plants and what they had in them and how to dose it out." Another of my friends had correspondents whom I met through the market bulletins, Ethel Harmon, wrote from South Carolina, "My mother made lots of sassafras tea in the spring of the year, and we had to drink it for our health and blood. She raised eight children of her own and two nieces. We had few doctor's bills then, so I feel her old remedies were useful to us."

Ever since the Indians taught the Spanish discoverers the medicinal properties of sassafras, it has been used in all parts of the country as a spring tonic and a home remedy for many ills. In the Lower South it is valued for a number of things, from keeping mites out of the chicken house to flavoring food. Mrs. Loudon in the *Lady's Companion to the Flower Garden* says the Choctaw Indians taught the Creoles to flavor their gumbo with filé, a yellow powder made from sassafras leaves. (In *Creole Sketches*, Lafcadio Hearn gives a recipe for Gumbo Filé, in which the ingredients are a whole chicken, a little ham, crabs or shrimp or both, oysters, dried okra, filé powder, and plenty of rice for thickening. It would be useless, he says, to give the proportions, for no two Creole cooks would agree.)

After the discovery of America, sassafras tea was long considered a cure-all. It was sold in the streets of London, after its introduction into England in 1633 or before. It soon became popular. Called saloop, and taken with milk and sugar, the tea was sold morning and evening to frequenters of The Gossipping Coffee House.

Sassafras, perhaps above almost any other plant, unites the original native Americans and the colonists, the North and the South, America and England, in the delight people had in it, the hope they placed in it for refreshment and for healing. William Bartram learned in the eighteenth century from Indians in New York that an eyewash made from the pith of the young shoots served a worthy purpose, and an old Swedish woman told him that she had learned soon after her immigration to cure people of dropsy by a decoction of sassafras root in water drunk every morning. Thoreau, on his solitary winter walks, liked to break a twig of green-barked sassafras root to smell. "I am always exhilarated, as were the early voyagers, by the sight of it," he wrote, "and I am startled to find it fragrant as in summer. It is an importation of all the spices of Oriental summers into our New England winter, very foreign to the snow and the oak leaves. The green leaves bruised have the fragrance of lemons and a thousand spices. To the same order belong cinnamon, cassis, camphor." Sassafras is mentioned in an old street song in *Creole Sketches*:

> Pitis sans papa, pitis sans maman,
> Qui ça vous z'aut' fé pou' gagnin l'arzan!
> Pou' fé di té n'a fouille sassafras,
> Pou' fé de li l'encr' n'a porte grain salgras (chou-gras),
> Et v'la comme ça ne te fé pou' l'arzan.

Hearn was afraid that the old Creole lore was disappearing, but "pure fresh gumbo filé" still appears in the "Bark, Roots, and Herbs" columns of the Louisiana market bulletin, along with sassafras roots and mamou roots.

Mamou is a contraction of mammouth, the French word for mammoth. It is the Acadian name for the native coral bean, *Erythrina herbacea*, which has enormous roots and bright red seeds the Choctaws called spirit beans. In the village of Mamou, in Evangeline Parish, and all through the bayou country, the descendants of the Acadians still brew a tea from its seeds and roots for the relief of colds and influenza. Seeds are preferred, and the medicine is not thought to be effective unless an odd number is used. The roots are used in a cough drop sold in local drugstores, or used to be. The coral bean is a beautiful shrub though somewhat invasive. It has cool gray leaflets borne in threes, slender spikes of carmine flowers, and scarlet seeds that keep their color and can be used for dried bouquets. It is native along the coast as far north as Wilmington. I once had a plant from Texas in my garden, but it did not persist.

Seeds of herbs are advertised in the market bulletins, "ten different kinds for ten cents and stamped envelope." From time to time there are offerings of seeds or rooted plants of anise, basil, borage, catnip, chives, dill, fennel, horehound, and lavender; of spearmint, peppermint, and "iced-tea mint"; of tansy and thyme; of "rosemary from George Washington's garden," and "a few ditney rootings." The dittany will not be the true dittany of Crete (*Origanum dictamnus*), but mountain dittany (*Cunila origanoides*), which is steeped in whiskey to make an aromatic drink that is good for colds.

*

Herb gatherers still roam the southern mountains as they did at the turn of the century when Mrs. Lounsberry and her illustrator, Mrs. Rowan, travelled by train, horse and buggy, and on foot, to study the mountain plants and learn their uses. In North Carolina, they went from cabin to cabin, always meeting with kindness and hospitality, but sometimes failing to draw the people out. The mountain people were shy and reticent and did not like being questioned about their deep feeling for the beauty around them. Mrs. Lounsberry's transports over acres of flame azalea in full bloom were met with the response that they were "pretty enough." She asked a taciturn mountaineer if the people loved their wildflowers. He replied, "No, Marm." Did they use any of the native plants to cure illnesses? "No, Marm." What did they do with them? "They lets 'em come and go."

While waiting for a train to take them up Roan Mountain, they climbed up the slope to pick branches of *Aralia spinosa* full of shining, black berries, and when the train suddenly appeared, they waved it down. On the train they met a "sympathetic, hypnotic, magnetic healer," who told them the berries they had picked were used to cure rheumatism.

✳

In the market bulletins herbs, roots, and barks are advertised by the boxful: half-gallon ice cream boxes, two- or four-pound lard boxes, "big soda box full of home grown sage cured in shade." One advertiser offers "a five-pound salt bag measured full."

The two most widely collected roots seem to be ginseng (*Panax quinquefolius*) and goldenseal (*Hydrastis canadensis*), sometimes shortened to "seng" and "seal." Ginseng is an Asiatic plant also native to North America. Its generic name comes from the Greek *panakos*, meaning cure-all or panacea, and both the Chinese and American Indians regarded it as a sovereign remedy for most diseases. The Chinese believed it would make the sick well and the well strong, relieve fatigue of body and mind, and even prolong life. They import it from this country, even though they regard the American kind as inferior to theirs, because their native species, *P. pseudoginseng*, has been virtually exterminated by root gatherers, although it still grows in Korea, which exports it into this country for sale to the Chinese communities in New York and on the West Coast.

André Michaux taught the people of the southern Appalachians to dig the root for export to China, but now there is little left for the diggers, as they did not take care to wait for the plants to go to seed first, even though I believe there is a law in North Carolina forbidding such premature digging, and even though Old Ned, a wise old black man who made his living around the turn of the century gathering roots and herbs, understood the need for conservation. His grandson, Ely Green, writing in *An Autobiography*, recalls what Old Ned said: "I have to go to the mountains as soon as the snow melts to get herbs. I have to make up some herbs for many people. The herbs I have are too dry. I will go to my herb beds and dig fresh ones. I want to teach you about herbs. Old Ned has to do a lot of things to help people."

He took Ely to Morgan Steep on a mountainside near Sewanee. "I have been getting my herbs here for thirty years," he said. "I always take some and leave some to grow more. This you must learn—not to destroy the growth of anything. You can make a living in the mountains if you learn the value of its gifts. Over there you see caltrop, catnip, hoorehound, and sasfras. . . . under the grapevine is a myrtle herb. The Indians believed in it. White people call it gensand. It is a medicine good for anything you suffer with. It sells for seven dollars a pound. These mountains is full of this kind of stuff." When he dug a plant, he pointed out that the root looked like a leg and that it was good for leg ailments—and then he put part of the root back in the ground.

Now rare in the wild, ginseng is advertised as plants and seeds in the market bulletins. Some sellers send free instructions; others charge extra for the advice. It takes three years for the seed to germinate, and they must be kept moist. The plants begin to fruit three years after they come up, but it is another five years before the roots are ready for the market.

The people of the mountains valued ginseng as a source of cash, but put little faith in it for their own medical purposes. Such is not the case with goldenseal, which is frequently advertised in the Alabama and Georgia bulletins by the local name, yellowroot. Early settlers learned its use from the Indians, and it has traditionally been highly regarded as a medicinal plant, of great advantage in treating nervous troubles when mixed with ginger.

The herb columns are rich in other roots of all sorts— mandrake root, squawroot, queen's root, Sampson's snakeroot, bloodroot, pleurisy root, comfrey root, and many more. Mandrake root is *Podophyllum peltatum* or may-apple, and may be listed under either common name in advertisements. The roots are collected in the fall and made into a laxative tea. It is said to be a dangerous home remedy, for roots and leaves are poisonous, and so are the fruits when green. Squawroot is sometimes *Mitchella repens*, the partridgeberry, sometimes *Caulophyllum thalictroides*, the blue cohosh, which is also called papooseroot and traditionally believed to be good for rheumatism, bronchitis, and colic. Queen's root or queen's delight is *Stillingia sylvatica*. I have seen it advertised only in the Alabama bulletin. Of it Mrs. Lounsberry wrote, "Very early in the spring many people sally forth quite oblivious to any other sensation than that of collecting queen's root to later use in medicinal ways." The ways were for treating skin diseases and kidney complaints. And of Sampson's snakeroot, Mrs. Lounsberry wrote that it was the mountain name for three different species of gentian, *Gentiana andrewsii*, *G. saponaria*, and *G. villosa*. "Decoctions made from them are taken in great doses as a remedy for dyspepsia and are favorably regarded as a powerful tonic to invigorate the system. . . . That the stuff has the effect of putting renewed life in them is true, but so little idea have they of the quantity that in other ways it causes them harm. They use it for their horses also. . . ." Bloodroot is in constant demand as a home remedy, especially for bronchitis. It is also called coon root, a corruption of the Indian name, puccoon. The Indians used the yellow juice for war paint and also to dye their baskets.

Pleurisy root (*Asclepias tuberosa*) and echinacea root are advertised from time to time in the Mississippi bulletin. Echinacea or coneflower is said to be good for ulcers and boils and blood poisoning. I have also read that it is an aphrodisiac. In the Georgia bulletin I found blackberry root advertised, which made me wonder, but sure enough Mrs. Grieve lists both American and English blackberry as medicinal plants, used as astringents. Alumroot (*Heuchera americana*), also an astringent, appears occasionally, and I have seen star root (*Aletris farinosa*) in the Alabama bulletin. Said to be somewhat narcotic, star root is also called colic root, ague root, and unicorn root. As for comfrey roots, they are in great demand not only in the rural South but also in other parts of the country. Both roots and leaves are used externally for sprain, swellings, bruises, and cuts.

The angelica root of the bulletins is the American species *Angelica atropurpurea*, used in this country as a substitute for *Angelica archangelica* and believed to have the same medical properties, though it is not so aromatic. All through the ages angelica has been considered a protection from contagion, witches, spells, and enchantments, and held in such reverence that it is called the Root of the Holy Ghost. John Gerard in *Leaves from Gerard* says it is a "singular remedy against poyson, and against the plague, and all infections taken by evill and corrupt aire; if you doe but take a piece of the root and hold it in your mouth, or chew the same between your teeth, it doth most certainly drive away the pestilential aire."

Mrs. Grieve considered poke root (*Phytolacca americana*) one of the most important plants native to America, and the advertisers in the bulletins seem to agree with her. "Set now," one says, "and have early healthful salad for years to come." Although the roots are advertised, they are only for planting. It is the tender young shoots that are eaten, the roots themselves being poisonous. "Human beings have been poisoned by eating parts of the roots with young green shoots as pot-herbs," Muenscher says in *Poisonous Plants of the United States*. "If the young shoots are cooked thoroughly and the water in which they are cooked is discarded, they make excellent greens or substitutes for asparagus. Children are sometimes poisoned by eating the berries . . . but the most poisonous part of the plant is the root. It has been used extensively in the preparation of certain drugs, and as a household remedy for skin diseases and rheumatism." Poke comes from pocan, the Indian name for the plant, and in the bulletins it is sometimes advertised as poke salit, a carryover from Elizabethan usage, in which salit covered potherbs as well as uncooked greens.

Some of the spellings of herbs—penneroil, heal oil, savage sage—remind me of Colette's account of La

Varenne, the village herb woman, in "For a Flower Album." La Varenne never got the plant wrong, but she seldom got its name right. She said "amourous" for "amurosis" ("and thus the ancient narcotic was turned into an aphrodisiac"), and like the rest of the village she called geraniums "geramions." When Colette was a child she loved to follow La Varenne into the fields because she said little and smelled of artemisia and winter mint. She told the little girl the uses of the simples, as they went along: "That's a cure for warts. . . . That kills dogs. . . . That's the serpent-herb; wherever you come across it, you'll always find a snake hard by."

Leaves are also advertised in the bulletins: sassafras, of course, and also sumac (sometimes spelled in the Elizabethan way as shoemake, a spelling that suggests the uses of the tannins in the plant to make leather), life-everlasting, and mullein. Another name for life-everlasting (*Gnaphalium obtusifolium*) is rabbit tobacco, and indeed, when I was growing up, children smoked it. Thoreau often spoke of the way the dead plants kept their scent in winter, "like the balm of the fields," and he said the refreshing aroma of the plants in summer was bracing to the thought. Mullein has its long traditions. It is now so thoroughly naturalized in this country that I forget it is not a native. The Romans taught the English its uses, and they must have brought the knowledge to America along with the plant. Like angelica, this is another herb that protects against enchantment: Ulysses carried a mullein plant to protect him against Circe.

The Georgia bulletin is rich in barks: birch, dogwood, sassafras, persimmon, wild cherry, wahoo, and wild cucumber. All parts of the persimmon are useful: the inner bark is a tonic, small articles are manufactured from the wood, the fruit can be made into persimmon beer, and the seeds have been roasted as a substitute for coffee. Wahoo is *Euonymus atropurpurea*, and the bark of the root is sold as well as the bark of the shrub. The bark of the cucumber tree (*Magnolia acuminata*) is used in a tonic. Mrs. Lounsberry says an infusion of the fruit in whisky or apple brandy is supposed to prevent intermittent fevers — or perhaps it just makes a good excuse for a drink?

Most of the herbs and barks in the Georgia bulletin seem to come from the mountains, especially a little town called Ellijay. The mountain people also advertise buckeyes. They consider them lucky. An extract made from them is believed to cure rheumatism. Even carrying a buckeye in your pocket, it is thought, will keep you free from rheumatic pains. One species, *Aesculus octandra*, is used to give the appearance of age, a caramel tone, to the clear raw whiskey some moonshiner has distilled in some deep ravine.

In the Georgia mountains, buckeyes are sold by the gallon.

Mrs. Harmon's Herbs

Advertisements for "a good start of ground ivy, a medicinal plant," often appear in the Georgia bulletin. The whole herb (*Glechoma hederacea*) is used, being gathered in May when it is in flower. This plant has a long history as a household medicine, as a tea for coughs and headaches and backaches, and as a salve for cuts and sprains and sore muscles. Some people have even thought, optimistically, that it was a source of eternal youth. It has as many folk names as it has uses: alehoof (because it improves the flavor of beer), hedgemaids, haymaids, and gill-go-over-the-ground (Gill—or Jill—meaning wench: "every Jack must have his Jill.") Mrs. Ethel Harmon has written me about the reputed wonders of ground ivy, and also sent her further notes on home remedies still used in her part of South Carolina. "We use partridgeberry as a medicine. All you have to do is to gather the vines, wash them good, and put about two cups of them into a two-quart jar. Keep in the refrigerator and drink from it. This is fine for female trouble. I feel like it has kept two of my neighbors out of the hospital. It is known as squaw vine, and was used by the Indians. We have plantain too. They say it is good for sores and sprains. Cocklebur tea is fine for bathing cow bags. It keeps down milk fever. Black-berry root is good for dysentary."

Thoreau often came upon the twin flowers of the par-tridgeberry (*Mitchella repens*) when he walked in the wood late in June or early in July. He found them in Deep Cut Woods, Laurel Glen, and Hubbard's Grove. Partridgeberry "so abundantly in bloom now in the northwest part of this grove, emits a strong, astringent, cherry-like scent which is agreeable to me as I walk over it." In my own garden it blooms—those years that it bothers to bloom —at the end of May, and it never fruits. It is also called twinberry because two little white flowers are joined together with one ovary.

As for plantain, its medicinal qualities were praised in ancient times, and I like to think of Mrs. Harmon's finding the same virtues in it that Pliny and Dioscorides found long ago. It has long been considered a wound herb.

Culpeper says, "All the plantains are good wound herbs to heal fresh or old wounds, or sore, either inward or outward." Romeo recommended it to Benvolio to treat a broken shin. One legend has it that it is useful to toads as well as men: eating a leaf fortifies a toad so that it will not be poisoned if bitten by a spider.

The broad-leafed plantain (*Plantago major*) has interesting folk names. It is called cuckoo's bread, because like the bird it is supposed to have mystical and prophetic powers. It is said once to have been a maiden who waited by the roadside for a lover who never came. Eventually she turned, like Narcissus, into a plant, but unlike Narcissus, she becomes a cuckoo every seven years. "The broad plantain," Peter Kalm wrote, "grows on the highroads, foot paths, meadows, and in the gardens in great quantity. Mr. Bartram had found this plant in many places on his travels, but he did not know whether it was an original American plant, or whether the Europeans had brought it over. This doubt had its rise from the savages (who always had an extensive knowledge of the plants of this country), pretending that it never grew here before the arrival of the White Man. They therefore gave it a name which signified the Englishman's foot, for they say that wherever a European has walked, it grows in his footsteps." The dried leaves of this plantain, incidentally, are sometimes advertised in the bulletins as "plantation."

Waybread, spelled various ways, was the name for plantain among the Saxons, who called it the "mother of worts."

Over thee carts creaked
Over thee Queens rode

Over thee brides bridalled
Over thee bulls breathed.
All these thou withstoodst
And with stound stayedst
As thou withstoodst
Venom and vile things
And all the loathly ones
That through the land rove.
Saxon Herbal (1588)

To the Saxons it was one of nine sacred herbs. In Christian symbolism it becomes the way to Christ, so that in Renaissance painting it is often found at the foot of the Cross. Since it is a roadside herb, it is not surprising to find it recommended in *The Good Housewife's Handmaid* (1588) as a remedy for feet sore from travel: "Take plantaine and stamp it well, and anoynt your feet with the juice thereof, and the greefe will swage."

Mrs. Harmon's good words for cocklebur tea as a bag balm are new to me, but in *A Modern Herbal* Mrs. Grieve says that the cocklebur (*Agrimonia eupatoria*) is a sure specific in hydrophobia and an active styptic, local and general. The whole plant is used.

The ancient Greeks prescribed blackberries for gout, and the Romans considered the roots boiled in wine an astringent. In England, cottagers believed that burns would be healed if blackberry leaves were laid on the affected part while this charm was read:

There came three Angels out of the East,
One brought fire and two brought frost;
Out fire and in frost;
In the name of the Father, the Son, and the Holy Ghost.

But these same cottagers considered blackberries poison-ous after Michaelmas day, when the Devil curses all of the bushes and spits on them.

It utterly fascinates me how much of the ancient lore still survives in the knowledge of my market-bulletin friends like Mrs. Harmon—and how much of it may be lost with them. My latest letter from her was not encouraging. Not having heard from her for some time, I wrote to ask how she was. "I am so glad to hear from you," she replied.

> I hope you are well and able to attend to your flowers. As for me I have been blocked. My husband had a heart attack in April, and is now in a nursing home in Saluda. My children don't want me to stay here alone, but that is where I find peace of mind. I am seventy-three years old, and have trouble with my legs and back. I can't ramble the woods to find wild flowers like I used to do. My children all tell me don't leave the yard. We have so many hard things to accept in life. I am almost in woods, can't see a light anywhere at night. I wish you could come down to see this part of the world, would love to have you and be able to ramble for wild flowers. We have lots of rambling ground. I have permission from the paper company that owns land near us to gather any flowers I want, if I had some one to keep me from getting lost in the woods.

Rattlesnake Masters

There is no telling how many kinds of plants the Indians of North America believed in as a cure for snakebite. I found more than two dozen under "rattlesnake" in the index of Britton and Brown's *Illustrated Flora*, and I am sure that numerous others could be added. The Indians called them rattlesnake masters.

According to the Doctrine of Signatures, the medicinal properties of plants were disclosed in their forms. Thus plants supposed to cure snakebite were often chosen for some fancied resemblance to snakes. This old tradition was brought to America by the earliest English settlers, and it has lingered long in the Appalachian highlands. To the mountain people, the finely cut lip of the beautiful yellow-fringed orchid (*Habenaria ciliaris*) looks like the forked tongue of a rattlesnake and the anther sacs like his fangs. The Indians must have operated somewhat along the lines of the Doctrine of Signatures themselves, for I have read that they thought that the lightly veined leaves of the downy rattlesnake plantain (*Goodyera pubescens*), which is also called adder's violet, looked like a snake's skin. I'm not quite sure what trust to put in the claim that they were so sure it would cure snakebite that they would deliberately let themselves be bitten, if the plant were at hand.

In writing about the plants used by the Indians, Robert Beverley, the first native historian of Virginia (*The History and Present State of Virginia*), said, "There's the Rattle-Snake-Root to which no remedy was ever yet found comparable; for it effectually cures the Bite of a Rattle-Snake, which sometimes has been mortal in Two Minutes. If this Medicine be early applied, it presently removes the infection, and in Two or Three Hours, restores the Patient to as perfect Health, as if he had never been hurt. This operates by violent Vomit; and sweat." This was probably *Aristolochia serpentaria*, the plant called Virginia snakeroot. It has fibrous, aromatic roots and curious little, dark, twisted flowers. It is also called sangrel snakeweed and black snakeroot, and its natural range is Connecticut southward to Florida and Louisiana. It has other names, and to confuse matters further, there are other, unrelated, plants called black snakeroot. The black snakeroot often listed in the various market bulletins is *Cimicifuga racemosa*. Another snakeroot is *Sanicula marilandica*, called sanicle from the Latin "sanus," pertaining to health or healing.

In the eighteenth century Dr. John Tennant, a Scot living in Pennsylvania, learned about seneca snakeroot (*Polygala senega*) from the Indians. Experimenting with this plant, which occurs from New Brunswick to Arkansas, he found it useful in treating pleurisy. It was called mountain flax by John Custis, who wrote Peter Collinson about a man who had a distemper "endemiall to Africk," which was cured by two purges from this plant, administered by a woman who came from England. For more than a year, he said, the man had remained in good health. "I have sent to you for some of the herb; which by God's leave I will take when I get it; and some of the seed to propagate; I am told it is as common and cheap with you as penny royall." I wondered why he would send to England for an herb native to eastern North America, but Collinson's reply, offering to send "the herb," illustrates the confusion that often accompanies identifying plants by their common names, for Collinson spoke of an entirely different genus than *Polygala*, though also native to America: "I think I have seed and raised plants of what you call Rattle Snake Root; I take it to be a species of Eringo or sea Holly."

The snakeroot of which Collinson wrote Custis would seem to be *Eryngium aquaticum*, whose flower heads are small, spikey globes. It has diuretic properties and was much employed by physicians in South Carolina during the nineteenth century in treating dropsy. I once had *E. aquaticum* in my garden, but its preferred habitat is damp pinelands, and it eventually succumbed in a very dry season. *E. yuccifolium*, whose swordlike leaves gave it its name, will tolerate dry, sandy soil.

There is also much confusion about the plants that are commonly called button snakeroot and Sampson's snakeroot.

Through one of the market bulletins, I briefly grew a button snakeroot that was a beautiful thistle, one I had never seen before. I was not able to identify it, for it died as soon as it bloomed and did not reseed. The root, set out in the fall, produced a wine-striped silvery winter rosette, and in the spring a thick stalk appeared with a handsome bouquet of large purple flowers. Another button snakeroot, from Miss Bessie Brown, an advertiser in the South Carolina bulletin, also arrived in the fall. It didn't survive the winter, so I couldn't identify it either. Still another button snakeroot, and traditionally considered a rattlesnake master in the southern mountains, is liatris or blazing-star, especially *L. spicata*.

Caroline Dorman told me that an old woman who worked for her said the closed gentian (*Gentiana andrewsii*) is Sampson's snakeroot; she said she sold herbs and had dug many a one. And Mrs. Lounsberry wrote, "All along the waysides going up Roan Mountain and following the road to Blowing Rock, we saw its small light blue flowers. Through these parts of the country the mountain people call it gall-flower because its juices are so bitter, and ague-weed on account of the extract they make from its roots and employ for curing fever." She says the closed gentian and also *G. saponaria* and *G. villosa*, the marsh gentian, all seem to be indiscriminately called Sampson's snakeroot throughout the mountains, as I have mentioned earlier. "Their 'yarb' doctors among them," she wrote, "make it into powders. The Negroes . . . have real faith that gentians can cure snakebite."

Congo root (*Psoralea psoraliodes*), a small legume native to Virginia and sometimes made into a tea, is yet another plant commonly called Sampson's snakeroot.

Another snakeroot is *Collinsonia canadensis*, listed in an advertisement in the Mississippi bulletin as "stonewort, cut up and dry." John Bartram discovered it and sent it to Europe, where Linnaeus named it for Peter Collinson, who well deserved the honor. Bartram held that it was an excellent remedy against all sorts of pain in the limbs and against a cold, when the parts affected were rubbed with it. Conrad Weiser, an interpreter for the Indians of Pennsylvania, reported that an Indian badly bitten by a rattlesnake recovered easily after drinking water in which *C. canadensis* had been boiled. And William Bartram wrote admiringly of it in his *Travels*: "It is diuretic and carminative, and esteemed a powerful febrifuge. An infusion of its tops is ordinarily drank at breakfast, and is of an exceedingly pleasant taste and flavour; when in flower, which is the time [it is gathered] for preservation and use, it possesses a lively aromatic scent, partaking of lemon and aniseed." Because of this scent, this plant is also called citronella, and it is one of several plants called heal-all.

In spite of all the miracles attributed to the rattlesnake masters, the mountain man will tell you that, as for himself, he would rather rely upon whisky. "People don't understand snakebite," Ray Hicks said when I visited him at Banner Elk. "There *are* herbs for it, but turpentine and whisky are the surest cures." He knows a man who has three scars on his face and twelve on his legs from being bitten when he was gathering ginseng. "He never goes where snakes are," Mr. Hicks explained, "without taking three bottles of turpentine and a pint of good pure whisky with him. When a snake strikes he pours the turpentine on the wound, a bottle at a time, until all of the poison is drawn out. Then he drinks the whisky, and lies down. If you drink the whisky first it will kill you."

The Pleasing Poppies

Some time ago, there was a discussion about the opium poppy (*Papaver somniferum*) in the "Straight Line" column of the Georgia bulletin. "I have been told," a reader wrote, "that some kinds of poppies are used for dope. I bought some seed in a local supermarket but don't want to grow something illegal." The answer was, "It is not illegal to grow poppies, as they are not harmful in their natural form. The poppy-seed capsules must be slashed and the juice collected and treated to produce heroin." According to federal law it is illegal, I still believe, to grow

P. *somniferum*, and I imagine that the poppy seeds sold commercially for cooking have been treated to keep them from germinating. Nevertheless, these poppies go from garden to garden, and they are widely advertised in the market bulletins in early summer. Sometimes they are incorrectly listed as Shirley poppies, and in all good faith, I feel sure, for I never heard of gardeners raising them for anything nowadays but their beauty. There were two offerings in the South Carolina bulletin, the issue of June 6, 1974. "Taking orders for annual and Shirley poppy seed, some almost as large as saucers, several colors including double red, purple, salmon, Iceland pink, others; lots double, some semi and singles. 1,000—50 cts. plus stamped addressed envelope." "Seeds, poppy, red-purple, pink, and assorted, 500 for ten cents."

P. *somniferum* has been grown in this country since colonial times. In the Moravian archives, it is on a list of plants growing in a medicinal garden in Old Salem in 1760. During the Civil War, Porcher felt its cultivation worthy of attention, and in 1872 did some research on the subject.

Under the order of the Surgeon-General, I was able to collect, in a few days, more than an ounce of gum opium, apparently of very excellent quality, having all the smell and taste of opium (which I have administered to the sick), from specimens of the red poppy found growing in a garden near Stateburg, S.C. I have little doubt that all we require could be gathered by ladies and children within the Confederate States, if only the slightest attention was paid to cultivating the plants in our gardens. It thrives well, and bears abundantly. It is not generally known that the gum which hardens after incising the capsules is then ready for use, and may be prescribed as gum opium, or laudanum and paregoric may be made from it, with alcohol or whisky.

At the same time, poppies were being grown in the North by the Shakers. "We always had extensive poppy beds," Sister Marcia Ballard says, "and early in the morning, before the sun had risen, the white-capped sisters could be seen stooping among the scarlet blossoms to slice the pods from which the petals had fallen. Again after sundown they came out with little knives to scrape off the dried juice."

Capsules of *P. somniferum* are in the *Dispensatory* as officinal in the United States. "Dried poppy-heads," Dr. Wood says, "though analogous to opium in medical properties, are exceedingly feeble. They are nevertheless asserted, in the form of decoction, to have proved fatal in a child. . . . They are sometimes employed in decoction, as an external emollient and anodyne application; and, in emulsion, syrup, or extract, are often used internally, in Europe, to calm irritation, promote rest, and produce generally the narcotic effects of opium." I don't think the market bulletin ladies use them for any purpose other than dried arrangements.

Gerard says, "The heads of Poppie boiled in water with sugar to a syrup cause sleep, and are good against rheumes and catarrhes that distil and fall down from the brain into the lungs."

The seeds are not narcotic, and they are valuable for their oil and for food. Porcher considered the oil the purest kind for the table "and the most agreeable that is known." Varieties with single flowers produce the largest pods, and the yield is improved if they are grown in deep, rich soil. Linnaeus counted 32,000 seeds in one pod, but I find it takes several of those in my garden to fill a tablespoon.

Opium poppies have been grown in many of the gardens on Ridgewood Avenue in Charlotte ever since we moved here, and seeds given to me twenty-five years ago still breed true. The wide flowers, to five inches across, are the China Rose of the Horticultural Color Chart, with a large, dark purple spot in the center. They have been gradually crowded out by encroaching perennials, and so escaped notice recently when police visited the street, and a neighbor was ordered to pull her poppies up.

Alice Morse Earle, who with John Ruskin was a great lover of poppies, wrote in *Old Time Gardens* that she vividly recalled "the horror of a visitor of antique years in our mother's garden during our childhood, when we were found eating poppy seeds. She viewed us with openly expressed apprehension that we would fall into a stupor." Mrs. Earle did not stop eating poppy seeds ("and very pleasant of taste they were"), but she found it reassuring when returned missionaries visiting her home told her that in the East poppy-seed cakes were a staple food. Mrs. Earle on the subject of poppies is really quite wonderful, so I will quote her further here. "There is something very fine about a poppy, in the extraordinary combination of boldness of color and great size with its slender delicacy of stem, the grace of the set of the beautiful buds, the fine turn of the flower as it opens, and the wonderful airiness of poise of so heavy a flower. The silkiness of tissue of the petals, and their semi-transparency in some colors, and the delicate fringes of some varieties, are great charms. . . . And when the flowers have shed, oh, so lightly! their silken petals, there is still another beauty, a seed vessel of such classic shape that it wears a crown."

Mrs. Earle was somewhat perplexed by the aversion the poppy met with in Elizabethan times, and by the way Parkinson stigmatized it as "Joan Silver-pinne, fair without and foule within," words whose meaning she found mysterious. I don't know about "foule within," but Joan was sometimes a pejorative term for a rough country woman, and the long-stalked pod does look something like a silver hat pin.

The Cordial Flowers

The cordial flowers are the ones that cheer the heart. There are many of these, but the cardinal ones are the rose, the violet, alkanet, and borage, borage being the foremost.

When I asked Mrs. James Anthony of Easley, South Carolina, with whom I sometimes exchange letters, whether she made use of borage, she wrote, "Yes, I have borage seed. I am going to plant it as soon as the ground warms up. Borage is used for a merry heart." Her words reflect a long and ancient tradition. Pliny the Elder says in the *Historia naturalis* that borage brings courage.

The herbalists found in borage properties to soothe as well as to stimulate. Pliny believed it to be Homer's nepenthe, the herb that brought forgetfulness. "Those of our time," Gerard said, "do use the floures in sallads, to exhilerate and make the mind glad. . . . Syrrup made of the floures of Borrage comforteth the heart, purgeth melancholy, and quieteth the phrenticke or lunaticke person. Syrrup made of the juice of Borrage with sugar, adding thereto pouder of the bone of a Stags heart, is good against swouning, the cardiacke passion of the heart, against melancholy and the falling sicknesse."

Although it is called *Borago officinalis*, borage is not officinal in the United States. Dr. Wood says it is scarcely known in this country as a medicinal plant, though much used in France for rheumatism, diseases of the skin, and other afflictions.

Borage is often combined with bugloss by the herbalists. Of all the cordial flowers, Robert Burton says in *The Anatomy of Melancholy*, bugloss "may challenge the chiefest place, whether in substance, juice, seeds, flowers, leaves, decoctions, distilled waters, extracts, oils, etc., for such kind of herbs be diversely varied. Bugloss is hot and moist, and therefore worthily reckoned up among those herbs which expel melancholy and exhilerate the heart. Pliny much magnifies this plant."

In the *Dispensatory*, bugloss (*Anchusa officinalis*) and alkanet (*Alkanna tinctoria*) are not officinal. There is too much confusion among writers both ancient and modern for me to thread my way among the arguments as to the identity of these plants, and so far as I know neither is made use of in the South. *Anchusa officinalis*, Dr. Wood says, is unknown in the United States, though "formerly much esteemed as a medicine. The root and flowers are officinal. . . . The plant has no claim whatever to the credit, formerly attached to it, of possessing cordial and exhilarating properties. It was used by the ancients in hypochondriacal affections; but, as it was given in wine, the elevation of spirits was probably due to the vehicle."

The market bulletins are silent about any medical properties of a cordial or any other nature belonging to the numerous old roses they list, but *Rosa centifolia* and *R. damascena* are in the *Dispensatory* as officinal in this country. These two, the cabbage rose and the damask—particularly the damask—were the ones the herbalists most used in their waters and oils and ointments. They used hips, buds, and petals, and the further back you go, the more ailments were cured by them. "Nother is so vertuous in medicyn," Bartholomaeus Anglicus wrote in 1495. "Among all floures of the world the floure of the rose is cheyf . . . an wythstondeth and socouryth by vertue agenst many syknesses and evylles."

"The distilled water of Roses is good for the strengthening of the heart, and refreshing of the spirits, and likewise for all things that require a gentle cooling," Gerard says.

> It mitigateth the paine of the eyes proceeding of a hot cause, bringeth sleep, which also fresh roses themselves provoke through their sweet and pleasant smell. Of like vertue are the leaves of these preserved in Sugar, especially if they be bruised with the hands, and diligently preserved with Sugar, and so heat at the fire rather than boiled. The Conserve of Roses . . . taken in the morning fasting, and last at night, strengtheneth the heart, and taketh away the shaking and trembling thereof, and in a word is the most familiar thing to be used for the purposes aforesaid.

The dog rose (*Rosa canina*) and other species are described in the *Dispensatory* as officinal in Great Britain. In Europe, Dr. Wood says, they are used in a confection "intended chiefly to be an agreeable vehicle for other medicines." But the herbalists knew many more uses. Pliny, who believed that the roots were a cure for hydrophobia, gave it its specific name, *canina*. Culpeper in his *Complete Herbal* said, "The Hips are grateful to the taste, and a considerable restorative, fitly given to consumptive persons; the conserve is proper to all distempers of the breast, and coughs and tickling rheums" and also "dries up moisture and helps digestion." And always the hips comfort the heart.

Sweetbriar is the poet's eglantine, *R. eglanteria*, which was brought to this country in the early days, and is now naturalized in the East. The English eglantine, Mrs. Earle points out in *Old Time Gardens*, was quickly established here in the gardens of New England, as we know from "a cheerful traveler named John Josselyn, a man of everyday tastes and much inquisitiveness, and the pleasing literary style which comes from directness, and an absence of self-consciousness." In *New England's Rarities Discovered* (1672), he published a list of the vegetables and flowers grown in American gardens, including "Sweet Bryer," as well as "Sparagus" and "Holly hocks." Both eglantine and dog roses grew in the garden of Mrs. Earle's great-aunt in Walpole, New Hampshire, in 1830. I find no mention of these in the market bulletins, but they have naturalized, although uncommonly, in the Carolinas.

Thoreau writes of finding eglantine in bloom as he walked "up railroad" at five o'clock on a June morning in 1854, along with *R. nitida* "along the edge of ditches" and *R. virginiana* (formerly *R. lucida*). He picked all three in bud, as their petals drop the second day, and when the flowers opened they filled with their perfume the room where he sat reading and writing.

Neither Porcher nor Dr. Wood mention these two native species or our own wild rose, R. *carolina*, which ranges all the way from Canada to Texas, as medicinal, but their hips, at least, are popular now for their high content of vitamin C. Miss Sara Hodges says those of the wild roses are preferable to those of the garden roses. She brought me a jar of jam made from small, red hips that were, she said, sweet and mealy, as good as black haws to eat out of the hand. She used the recipe in Euell Gibbons' book *Stalking the Healthful Herbs*, which calls for seeded rose hips, sugar, and lemon juice, mixed in the blender.

"Pink violets blooming now" were advertised in the Georgia bulletin of October 24, 1973. I sent for them, they arrived in bloom, and they were, as I felt sure they would be, *Viola odorata* 'Rosina'. Planted in the garden, they did not bloom long, even though full of buds, because we had unusually severe early frosts, but they bloomed freely the next spring, starting in April. Other forms of *V. odorata* exist in old gardens in the South. Caroline Le Conte Gibbes sent me flowers of one of these after a visit to her brother and sisters at their country place where they grew, near Columbia, South Carolina. "I happen to be the most active of the Le Contes—82, 84, 85, 97," she wrote. "Have you the little old-fashioned English violets? I think red spiders have destroyed them everywhere in the world, except a few that my mother fought, bled, and died to save. I picked a few to put in this letter to show you what they are, and you must have a few roots if you have none. There were wide borders of them in all the gardens that I remember as a child."

Fortunately, they were not the last in the world, for not long afterward Mittie Wellford, a friend from Chance, Virginia, took me to two gardens in Virginia where they still flourish: her grandmother's at Montrose, near The Plains, and Barbara Richardson's, at Brookbank, near the Rappahannock River. I think they may be the variety praecox, which the R.H.S. *Dictionary of Gardening* describes as quite early. The flowers are very small, very pale, and very sweet.

Violets are as old as gardens, and as dearly loved. They are little herbs in substance, Anglicus says, but "the littlenesse therof in substance is noblye rewarded in greatness of savour and of vertue." Gerard, who called *V. odorata* the March violet, says, "The flowers are good for all inflammations, especially of the sides and lungs; they take away all hoarseness of the chest." According to him, they also cure headache, bring on restful sleep, and even bring moral benefits, in that they "admonish and stir up a man to that which is comely and honest."

All four of these cardinal cordial flowers go into metheglin, which is mead, the traditional drink of Wales, with spices added. Great handfuls of sweetbrier, violet flowers and leaves, bugloss, borage, rosemary, strawberry leaves, and many other herbs and spices, including a race of ginger (a race is a root), are boiled in water. After straining, honey is added and the mixture fermented with alebarm, a sort of yeast. They say it is heady stuff, and I feel sure it warms the heart.

In addition to these four main cordial herbs, Burton and others considered basil, rosemary, and many other plants comfort for the heart. Parkinson says the physical properties of ordinary basil are to "procure a cheerful and merry heart." About basil, Culpeper is at his best:

This is the herb which all authors are together by the ears about, and rail at one another, like lawyers. Galen and Dioscorides hold it not fitting to be taken inwardly, and Chrysippus rails at it with downright Billingsgate rhetoric. Pliny and the Arabian Physicians defend it. . . . And away to Dr. Reason went I, who told me it was a herb of Mars, and therefore called basilicon, and it is no marvel if it carry a kind of virulent quality with it. Being applied to the place bitten by venomous beasts, or stung by a wasp or hornet, it speedily draws the poison to it. . . . Every like draws its like . . . and it helps the deficiency of Venus in one kind so it spoils her action in another.

Basil is the common name of the genus *Ocimum*. Common or sweet basil does not get its specific name, *basilicum*, from the Latin *basilicus*, as an antidote to the poison of the basilisk, but from a Greek word meaning royal. It is not officinal. Dr. Wood says that basil has "the ordinary properties of the aromatic plants." Mrs. Grieve says it has been used for mild nervous disorders and for the alleviation of wandering rheumatic pains; the dried leaves, in the form of snuff, are said to be a cure for nervous headaches. In the South, basil is used mostly, perhaps entirely, for cooking.

In the sixteenth century Paracelsus praised lemon balm (*Melissa officinalis*) as a renewer or restorer of youth. Some of the women who advertise it in the market bulletins make the same claim exactly, causing me to wonder by what precise chain the old herbal wisdom has passed down to the rural South. If it does not renew my youth, at least for the moment it lifts my spirits, and I agree entirely with Burton about this sharp, sweet herb:

"Nothing better for him that is melancholy than to steep this and borage in his ordinary drink."

Both seeds and plants of rosemary appear in the South Carolina bulletins from time to time, but not as often as some of the other herbs. It was brought to New England in the seventeenth century, but John Josselyn noted that it was unsuited to the harsh climate. I have not discovered that it is used medicinally as a cordial in the South, but to the herbalists it was one of the most important of all plants. "The Arabians and other Physitions succeeding," Gerard said, "do write that Rosemary comforteth the braine, the memorie, the inward senses, and restorest speech unto them that are possessed with the dumbe palsie." His fellow herbalist Parkinson considered rosemary "almost of as great use as Beays, or any other herbe both for inward and outward remedies, and as well for civill as physicall purposes. Inwardly for the head and heart; outwardly for the sinewes and joynts; for civill uses, as all doe know, at weddings, funerals, and to bestow among friends."

Some years ago I sent for a list of plants from a gardener in the Midwest, and one plant intrigued me particularly: the toper's plant. It took me some time to discover that this is an old name for salad burnet (*Poterium sanguisorba.*) This folk name is not in the O.E.D., which is strange, since Anne Pratt is often quoted by its editors and it was in her *Flowering Plants, Grasses, Sedges, and Ferns of Great Britain* that I found it. This burnet, Miss Pratt says, "seems to be that which has acquired so much celebrity as the toper's plant, for it was customary to infuse it in various liquors, and with borage and some flowers it helped to compose that celebrated beverage called a cool tankard." Of salad burnet, which came to this country at least as early as 1621 when Robert Hill, grocer, sent a bill for "an ounce of Burnett" to John Winthrop the Younger and which Mrs. Eugene Polsfuss of Macon occasionally advertises in the Georgia bulletin, Culpeper says that it is "a most precious herb" and that the "continual use of it preserves the body in health and the spirit in vigour." "The greatest use the Burnet is commonly put unto," Parkinson says, "is to put a few leaves into a cup with Claret wine, which is presently to be drunke, and giveth a pleasant taste thereunto, very delightful to the palate, and is accounted a helpe to make the heart merrie."

Gerard is more succinct: "It gives a grace in the drynkynge."

The Private Bulletins

Joe's Bulletin

The market bulletins are free to anyone who asks for them, but no out-of-state advertisements are accepted. For the rest of the country, several little magazines and trade papers serve to bring buyers and sellers and traders of plants together. They carry classified advertisements and articles written by their readers and advertisers.

One such paper is *Joe's Bulletin* ("The Market Place for the Nation's Small Flower Growers"), published monthly in Lamoni, Iowa. Joe Smith published it for nearly fifty years, but a few years ago it was taken over by Jack Terry. Recently the bulletin reprinted the autobiography Joe Smith wrote for it some twenty years earlier. He says he was very small when his parents homesteaded in the "bunch grass country" in the state of Washington. He rode the range as a boy, but turned to journalism after college. He enlisted in the army during the Spanish-American War to avoid arrest after he called a superior court judge "a legal light without legal knowledge and a judge without judgment." When he returned from the Philippines, with a wound and a decoration for bravery, he continued to campaign against dishonesty in high places. "I was once arrested for criminally libelling the mayor of Seattle," he says, "but the jury didn't think so." He rode on Theodore Roosevelt's special train when the president toured Washington in 1903, "and personally conducted President Taft on a similar tour in 1908." He wrote a story that caused the president of the Northern Pacific Railroad to lose his job.

All this time Joe paid no attention to flowers. He didn't know a black-eyed susan from a bachelor's button. It was only after he had been "fired from every leading newspaper in Washington" that he took up flower growing. He planted irises and peonies and gladioluses. One year he grew a hundred thousand delphiniums. Someone at the Department of Agriculture aroused his interest in bulbs. He planted a million daffodils; the bulletin started out as his bulb catalog. His bulb business was a great success, but he got so tired of it that it was a relief when the depression wiped him out. From then on, he collected and distributed flower seed, sending out the bulletin free, until the circulation reached six thousand and costs forced him to charge for subscriptions.

Joe died in 1962, but the bulletin still shows his mark. In nearly every issue there is a letter from one of his old friends. After his death, Mrs. Cecil Ritchey wrote:

> I have taken Joe's Bulletin from way back, and had a lot of flowers—swaps, sell or giveaways. When the quarantine was on Dutch bulbs, Joe got me started in bulb growing, advising me to dig the "Cats and

Dogs," as he called the bulbs on abandoned home-
steads. We gathered them by the wagonload. Joe
swapped me a peck of mixed bulbs for the same
amount of Cats and Dogs. Before the quarantine lifted
I was the only bulb grower in my state having inspec-
tion both spring and fall. After my husband died, I
went to make my home with my son in California,
but Arkansas called me back home, where I can dig
in the dirt when I please. . . . I am 83 and no longer
an active flower grower, but still have flowers.

"Joe was a sort of horticultural missionary, the Johnny
Appleseed of the flower world," says the bulletin's present editor, David DeLong. "He distributed, free or at cost,
over a million packages of seeds and thousands of plants
and bulbs. He hated dishonest or misleading advertising,
and he always insisted that bulletin advertisers offer mer-
chandise only under a guarantee of satisfaction or money
back, which is still required. Every advertiser is expected
to live up to it faithfully."

I thought of this expectation when I came across an
advertisement for seed of a tree now growing in New
Jersey, an "orange tree hardy in southern New England."
That can't be true, I thought, but reading further I real-
ized that it is. The plant advertised is *Poncirus trifoliata*,
commonly called the hardy orange, which bears, as the
advertiser says, "small golf-ball size oranges, not edible."
It is hardy in coastal Massachusetts, although it grows
only to six feet, about half the height it attains in the
South. In New England it blooms in April, but in Charlotte I look for the sweet, ethereal flowers in mid-March,
when they bloom in back streets and alleyways. (No one
thinks of planting them in gardens.) In September I watch

for the aromatic fruits to color. A hardy orange was considered a great thing when *P. trifoliata* was introduced into England from northern China in the middle of the nineteenth century. "If you'll provide the husband, I'll provide the orange blossoms," Canon Ellacombe liked to tell the unmarried women of his parish, when he showed them the celebrated specimen in the vicarage garden at Bitton (*In My Vicarage Garden*).

In spite of the legacy of Joe Smith's high standards, there are occasional complaints in the letters to the editor. "My garden is full of plants I've obtained over the years from your advertisers," writes an Iowa reader. "A few have not been up to expectation, but I count most of them as posy friends."

*

Hazel Maynard, who frequently advertises perennials from her garden in Fremont, Michigan, complains that plants are sometimes misnamed. "Heleniums are sent for Shasta daisies, and many hybrid iris are not correctly labelled. We all make mistakes, but I feel the seller should have correct names before advertising."

I asked for Mrs. Maynard's perennial list, and found it most interesting. I am ordering the mole plant (*Euphorbia lathyris*), not because I have any moles—what I need is a chipmunk plant—but because I just read that Will Ingwersen (*The Wisley Book of Gardening*) in England finds it delightful for its architectural qualities. Since he allowed it to colonize in his garden he has been untroubled by moles, but he warns that it is a terrific seeder and that the extra seedlings, though only biennials, must be destroyed before their deep-seated roots take hold. On Mr. Ingwersen's recommendation, I am also ordering *E. myrsinites*, for a sunny spot on the drywall, where he says it will be hardy, permanent, and beautiful (and not, I hope, invasive) and E. *epithymoides* (formerly E. *polychroma*), a virtually unknown plant which stands up well in comparison with any other spring-flowering plant. All it asks for is good drainage and full sun.

I have never seen plants of *Coreopsis verticillata* listed before. Mrs. Maynard describes this southern wildflower that grows as far north as Michigan and as far west as Nebraska as a "fern-leaved upright plant that resembles a kochia with yellow daisies." *Gaura lindheimeri*, another southern wildflower that she grows, is little cultivated in this country, although several English seedsmen list it, as does Jelitto, of Hamburg, West Germany. I used to have it in my Raleigh garden, where I did not think the little, white butterfly flowers were pretty enough to make up for the coarseness of the plants, but perhaps I did not do it justice: I grew it in shade, on clay, and it wants sun and a sandy soil.

Mrs. Maynard grows a goodly number of sedums. There are some gems among them, she says, and even some of the invasive ones may be useful, especially if they are evergreen: "Many are beautiful in bloom and equally so in winter when the foliage tints red, blue, violet, or pink." She favors gray-leaved plants: *Achillea filipendulina* 'Cloth of Gold,' *Alyssum murale*, several artemisias, a number of thymes, lavender, *Stachys byzantina*, and the gray santolina (*Santolina chamaecyparissus*) as well as the green (*S. virens*). She grows several rare salvias: *Salvia pratensis*, *S. hians*, and even *S. argentea*, the beautiful silver sage of the Mediterranean region, which has white flowers and large, handsome leaves covered with a deep, silver pile. Finding it hard to believe that lavender, santolina, and thyme were growing outside in Michigan in winter, I wrote to ask Mrs. Maynard if she moved them indoors. She wrote back to say no.

> I have santolina outside. Lavender and thyme grow outside too. In fact, I am leaving a rosemary, and ismene, and some tuberoses in the garden this winter, just to see what will happen. Last year we had a low of 35° below zero but 10° below is more usual. The snow cover of from three to six feet, which we have from early winter until spring, is a nice warm blanket. In our sandy soil there is not enough nitrogen present to make the lush growth of plants in heavy soil. We have full sun and good drainage and not too much rain for lavender and thyme.

It is, I think, worth mentioning that one of the great virtues of carrying on correspondence with people in various parts of the country who sell plants through the bulletins is that one learns that some of the advice in the standard books on gardening does not correspond to the actual experience of gardeners, who often succeed in raising plants that aren't supposed to do well in their particular climates.

*

Frances Holford of Quincy, Illinois (Zone 5), advertises seeds of hybrid gerberas. "Grow indoors," she says, "or out of doors with an eight-inch mulch of straw." She also lists an eggplant called Japanese Golden Eggs ("for the house or as an outdoor novelty") and *Atriplex hortensis* ("with ornamental violet foliage"). Japanese Golden Eggs turned out to be the yellow-fruited form of the tomato eggplant, *Solanum integrifolium*, commonly called love apple, an annual easily raised from seed, one whose fruits vary in color and shape, and one that generally comes equipped with vicious thorns. *Atriplex hortensis* is an ancient potherb, called orach or mountain spinach, frequently mentioned in English cookbooks of the fifteenth century and reported to have medicinal uses in reducing throat inflammation. There are three kinds: green, white, and red. The green and the white are best for the pot, but the red is a garden ornamental that was once popular for bedding. It is an annual, and Miss Holford says that seeds should be sown in spring—but here in the Southeast they can also be sown in fall for winter color.

*

From time to time, Pearl Beals of Chetek, Wisconsin, offers seed of the vesper iris, *Iris dichotoma* (now reclassified as *Pardanthopis dichotoma*), which is easily grown. Some will bloom the first year, but it is best treated as a biennial as they often bloom themselves to death in a season. Ella McKinney said in *Iris in the Little Garden* that she once kept a plant for three years. It grew to a height of five feet, and one summer she counted seventy-five flowers. It was in a part of the garden where the tea tray was carried in the afternoon, at the iris's brief hour of bloom. The flowers opened in shadow, "many at once with the effect of a floating lavender mist." The small and fleeting flowers bloom in August and September, long after the other irises have bloomed and faded.

*

Old varieties of vegetables are sometimes advertised in *Joe's Bulletin*. Sigurd Skorseth, who lived in Park Rapids, Minnesota, used to advertise "mother's green beans

—vigorous pole beans, tender, sweet, mellow, and nut-like in flavor. A continuous crop is borne from early summer to frost." They had been handed down in his family from one generation to the next for 150 years, and he thought them to be superior to the newer varieties on the commercial market. Now he is dead, and I wonder if some of his customers have thought to save the seed and preserve the strain.

*

Stella Skiba specializes in New Hampshire wildflowers and sends a free packet of seeds along with her list of some hundred and fifty roadside, meadow, and woodland plants, including native ferns and native shrubs with berries beloved by birds. Her shrubs include elderberry, steeple bush, dog rose, pasture rose, and swamp rose. Despite its name, the swamp rose (*Rosa nitida*) will grow in dry places as well as wet. She lists stitchwort, jewel-weed, and lady's thumb. Lady's thumb is *Epilobium angustifolium*, generally known as fireweed because it is one of the first plants to appear in areas that have been burnt over or bombed. It is adventive in this country, where it has become so widespread that it has taken on a number of local names such as black-heart, lover's-pride, and blooming sally. Garden books from the early herbals onward warn that it is extremely invasive. In my garden, far from being troublesome, I find that it blooms and disappears.

Through the bulletin, lots of plants from southern gardens travel northward. "I have received a shipment of carefully packed plants from the Deep South," writes Charles Humphryville, "and they have all taken up residence in Ohio and seem satisfied with their new home."

A number of my old friends from the Mississippi Market *Bulletin* also advertise in *Joe's Bulletin*. Mrs. Stamps of Bogue Chito offers seed of Indian corn ("five inches long, tiny cob, long yellow grain"), the Virginia rose, and washbowl pinks. Mrs. J. M. Apperson of Union has achimenes and thirty varieties of cannas, and Mrs. Radau of Saucier has native trees and shrubs.

*

One of the most faithful advertisers in *Joe's Bulletin* is W. O. Freeland of The Garden Spot in Columbia, South Carolina, who is always turning up with something new and rare. One of the rarest and most delightful is a male form of butcher's-broom (*Ruscus aculeatus angustifolius*), a little bristling shrub from the Middle East with bright green stalks and tiny tapered cladodes, much smaller and narrower, as the varietal name suggests, than the type. He traded it to me for the hermaphrodite form, which pleased him because of its pretty fruits, green and red on the bush at the same time.

Mr. Freeland has a collection of liriopes. He wrote me that the pure white one came from the Bishop's Garden at the National Cathedral in Washington. "It has multiplied nicely, and we have it at the foot of a low wall which is covered with creeping fig. The leaves of the variety latifolia are the widest of all, sometimes an inch across, and have an inclination to twist. The variety Christmas Tree came from the National Arboretum. The inflorescence, made up of very light violet flowers, has auxiliary spikes at the base, which give it the appearance of a little tree." Mr. Freeland also collects ivies. "So many people write about ivies without having enough acquaintance with the various clones," he says. "They know only baby clones grown in Northern greenhouses where development is arrested at a tender age, and they do not know that some sports soon revert to type when given optimum conditions. What we consider a fine ivy is a plant that is most beautiful after three years of vigorous growth. Green Ripples, Ray's Supreme, Fleur, Mander's Crested, crenata, and palmata are a few of our pets."

Along with advice about ivies, Mr. Freeland sends glimpses of his garden. "There have been some highlights this late summer," he wrote one September.

> *Lycoris squamigera* gave over fifteen bloom stalks, the first in three years, and they came at a cool, overcast time and had more blue in them than usual. Then the gloriosa lily ripened pods that burst to show the scarlet seeds, and *Manettia cordifolia glabra* climbed high into the Lady Banksia roses before showing its red flowers. But flowering plants are not all. A deeply shaded spot where no flower would ever bloom has given us a great amount of pleasure by just being green and cool. Over the years some aspidistras planted against the fence have thickened into great clumps, forming a fine background for our collection of rohdeas. *Rohdea marginata*, with white-edged wavy leaves is in a clump at one side, a single plant of R. *multifolia*, with triple white crest, is in the center, and a large group of dark green R. *japonica* finishes the planting. Last spring we planted Gold Band wandering Jew among the rohdeas, and it has filled the spaces between the dark green plants with bright yellow. If you should be overrun with something nice, please let us have a start.

*

Joe's Bulletin offers plants from all parts of the country: jacarandas from California, camellias from the Gulf Coast, cacti from Texas, palms from Florida, and passion vines from Tennessee "with recipe for delicious passion fruit marmelade." The advertisers, like those of the market bulletins, have their reasons for selling. "Husband's passing causes close-out of gloxinias." "Have to move, due to old age; offer holds good until everything is sold." "Need cash, must sell coleus collection." Trading goes on, too. One gardener says "Send what you have, I'll send what I have." Floriene Counts will exchange a dahlia bulb for an Indian-head penny and a five-cent stamp. Mrs. Miller will trade Stoke's aster for pink magic lily. Mrs. Allen, who has over three hundred varieties of iris, would like to trade with other collectors. And Mrs. Smalley would like to trade sheet music for bulbs and perennials. She has, it seems, just sold her piano.

The Garden Gate

I was distressed when The Garden Gate ("America's Largest Newspaper for Growers") ceased publication and turned its subscribers over to Joe's Bulletin. In it I found information that I never found elsewhere, and I miss it.

The Garden Gate was made up entirely of classified advertisements: roses from Texas, shallots from New Jersey, seeds of the old-time banana muskmelon from West Virginia, and from Arizona "four varieties of Hopi Indian beans (of superior taste) and six pure colors of corn, organically grown for centuries in the Painted Desert."

In the "Herbs and Roots" column I found Jerusalem artichokes from Michigan, sassafras from Ohio, and tansy from New York and elsewhere. Tansy seems to be the herb most generally in use all over the country. *The Garden Gate* advertised both seeds and plants, and "a package of dried tansy with recipes for tansy bread, rolls, and cookies." I had no idea that tansy was still used so widely in cooking, although it is a common herb at the curb market, and an herb with much history attached to it, both in Europe and America. In eighteenth-century England, Eleanour Sinclaire Rohde says, tansy pancake was as customary as roast goose at Michaelmas or gooseberry tart at Whitsun. In *A Garden of Herbs*, she gives an old recipe. The batter was made of flour, cream, eggs, and powdered sugar, then seasoned with the juice of spinach and tansy and a little grated nutmeg. The pancakes were fried in fresh butter and garnished with Seville oranges cut in quarters. In this country, tansy was among the simples that the early colonists brought with them. In her book about eighteenth-century life in a New England town, *The Salt-Box House*, Jane Shelton wrote that "tansy was not exactly a cure-all, but so potent that in spring, when the leaves were small and tender, it was served in tansy pancakes, which the children did not altogether dislike." I doubt whether I could eat anything flavored with tansy, but I like to think that there are still those who do.

Some time ago in *The Garden Gate* Lillian Petras of Hiram, Ohio, advertised jewels of Opar (*Talinum paniculatum*), an old-fashioned annual that is a great favorite in the southern market bulletins. I had never heard of its growing in the North, so I wrote Miss Petras to ask how it fared in her Zone 5 garden. She replied,

I was a little surprised to see a letter from someone I did not know, but then I found you are interested in flowers, so here is the answer. I did plant Jewels of Opar three years ago. I started the seed in a small pot in February (or about that time), then put the seedlings in larger pots, and in June transplanted them into the garden. They grew so large they took over the border. The tiny pink florets open only in the afternoon, but the seed pods are little orange balls that make the plant very ornamental. The seed dropped to the ground, and the following year the place was thick with plantlets. I transplanted them into all the empty spots. I grew tired of them and did not bother to plant any more, but a few seedlings come up each spring. They are enough.

Like Miss Petras, I am tired of jewels of Opar, and if a few seedlings come up each spring they will be enough.

Through *The Garden Gate* I met Mrs. Tate, who lives nearby in Belmont, a suburb of Charlotte. One rainy afternoon in April, when iris and wisteria were in bloom, a friend and I went to see her. We found her living alone, with flowers for companions—flowers everywhere, indoors and out. I had already written to Mrs. Tate about the Oriental rose which she advertised, and she had sent me some roots. It is *Calystegia hederacea*, a little, double pink morning glory, grown in some gardens as creeping verbena. It isn't anything like a verbena, but it does creep —below ground as well as above—and so, even though the flowers are sterile, it is a giveaway plant and must be watched. In some places in the South it has escaped from gardens to become a troublesome weed. In the North, I understand, there is no trouble with its getting out of bounds. Mrs. Tate also grows climbing okra, a vegetable that frequently appears in the market bulletins, and she says the tender young pods are very good when fried. It is not an okra, but one of the luffas or dishcloth gourds. Dried pods, with the seeds taken out and the skin removed, are sometimes sold as sponges.

Old-fashioned violets, as well as some modern ones, were regularly advertised by The Vista Violet Farm in Vista, California, whose proprietors, Chris and Mignon Jenkyns, publish a delightful brochure describing their plants. I was overjoyed to find that they sell a few species, in addition to the cultivated varieties of *Viola odorata* they offer, so I ordered several, including *V. lovelliana*, "an early bloomer with strong, lasting perfume." The plants arrived in good condition after their long trip across the country, comfortably packed in rosemary branches and accompanied by tips on raising violets—"mulch and water well in hot climates; winter in a cold frame or cover with several inches of straw in cold ones; dig in a bit of soil sulphur twice yearly; fertilize with sheep manure, oak-leaf mold, and fish emulsion for abundant bloom." There were also recipes for using the leaves of *V. odorata* as potherbs and in soups and salads, and for using the flowers in syrups and candies and teas, as well as to lend fragrance and color to vinegar.

In her cold garden in Appleton, Wisconsin, in Zone 4, Mrs. Seehawer grows "the good old weekday blossoms, ready and glad to bud and blow." In *The Garden Gate* she advertised "sundrops for golden color, tradescantias, brideflowers, and a hundred other northern-grown flowers that come up every year." Brideflowers are the double form of *Achillea ptarmica*, the traditional bouquet for bridesmaids in some parts of England. One of its country names is seven-years'-love. In Wisconsin tradescantia is called widow's-tears, Mrs. Seehawer told me when I wrote to ask her about Wisconsin names. Firecracker plant is *Monarda didyma*, or bee balm, and whispering charlie is *Aegopodium podagraria*, or bishop's weed. Widow's-tears is an old English name, but in Wisconsin *Lychnis coronaria* is known as bloody mary, while the English call it bloody william. Many familiar names appear on the Seehawer list, but there are two that I have never heard before: king flower and sun wheel. King flower is the coneflower, *Echinacea purpurea*. Sun wheel is the oxeye, *Buphthalum salicifolium*, a yellow daisy that grows on the subalpine slopes of southern Europe.

Seehawer's Garden is one of the few sources I know for the plume poppy (*Macleaya cordata*, known in cultivation as bocconia), a monumental plant with white stems and large, deeply lobed leaves that are pale green on top and snow white underneath. In summer, usually July with me, there are enormous plumes, up to three feet long, of tiny, creamy flowers like a fine spray. These are followed by flat seed pods in tones of celadon and fawn. I would not be without it, but it gives me more trouble than any plant in the garden. It has a strong tap root, which, as Mrs. Earle said in *Old Time Gardens* "would be a good symbol of the root of the tree Ygdrassyl—the Tree of Life, that never dies. You can go over the borders with scythe and spade and hoe, and even with manicure scissors, but roots of the Plume Poppy will still hide and send up vigorous growth the succeeding year." Mrs. Earle may have understated the matter slightly, for this plant seeds itself with abandon. The seedlings even come up in the cracks of cement pavement, and grow to their full height of five feet or more. I cannot imagine allowing it in a border, but it is a fine thing at the end of one of the garden paths, where by eternal vigilance I manage to keep it somewhat under control.

The Garden Gate, like the market bulletins and the other publications that bring amateur gardeners together, had its own flavor, and I was sorry when it ceased to be. But it left me richer in flowers and friends, and I must be grateful for this blessing.

Ozark Gardens

Many of my friends of the market bulletins, *Joe's Bulletin*, and *The Garden Gate*, patronize *Ozark Gardens*, a monthly newspaper published by Edna Bestard of Eureka Springs, Arkansas, and advertised as the only garden paper of its kind. It covers

> home life, the lure of the Ozarks, flowers, trees, and shrubs. It stresses healthful organic methods, champions humane practices, and urges conservation of all natural resources. It originates in, and breathes, the friendly informal spirit of the beautiful, still uncrowded regions of hills and valleys, but circulates widely in every state of the Union, every province of Canada, and several foreign countries. Every gardener will find something along the line of his special interest in the regular columns on African violets, orchids, cactus, lilies, begonias, daylilies, gourds, herbs, tropicals, wild flowers, unusual house plants, birds, and bonsai. Gardeners from everywhere

write of their actual experience. There are ads, swaps, free requests.

One of the regular contributors is Joe Mansfield, a Michigan gardener, who writes about people. Once he wrote about his neighbor, Gerhardt Neuhause, who lives alone on a hilltop near the village of White Cloud. Mr. Neuhause goes only where his bicycle takes him, talks more to flowers than to people, and can walk without being heard, see without being seen. He hybridizes daylilies, but he doesn't sell them, although he sells other plants from his nursery. He keeps the daylilies for his own enjoyment. One of his creations is named Minnie Morgan, for an Indian princess who once lived near White Cloud. She was very beautiful, Mr. Neuhause says, and so is the flower he named for her.

Sometimes Mr. Mansfield writes of people I already know about. One is C. W. Wood, whose garden notes I have followed for many years in various horticultural magazines, including *Ozark Gardens*. We have exchanged many letters about plants, and he finds out-of-print garden books for me. If he has a book in stock he sends it right on, even if the customer is unknown to him, and collects later. "I never worry about being paid," he says. "All flower lovers are good, honest, conscientious people. In my sixty years of experience, I have never been disappointed." His attitude reminds me that one of our fellow Brothers of the Spade, Peter Collinson, claimed back in the eighteenth century that he "never knew an instance in which the pursuit of such pleasure as the culture of a garden affords, did not either find men temperate and virtuous, or make them so."

Gardeners from all over the country contribute regularly to *Ozark Gardens*, but there are always comments on the progress of the seasons in the Arkansas countryside. If the winter is mild, buds of the Ozark witch hazels begin to color in December and come into bloom on the creek banks early in the New Year. Soon afterwards the burning bushes or flowering quinces (*Chaenomeles*) are ablaze in dooryards, and *Jasminum nudiflorum*, the winter jasmine, covers the fences with yellow stars. In early spring when bloodroot blooms with the sarvis trees, redbuds show pink and the scent of the balm-of-Gilead buds is like incense on the air. As summer nears, pink rain lilies, locally called naked ladies, bloom after fresh and sudden showers. Robins eat the elderberries, and the rain crow, called the thunderbird in the Ozarks, is believed to cry out three times at the coming of a thunder storm. During Indian Summer, according to country lore, little roadside asters bring good luck to lovers. And then, when the year comes to an end, there are hips and haws in the hedgerows and along the worn old stone fences.

One of the contributors to *Ozark Gardens* is Florence Knock. Mrs. Knock and I began to exchange letters and plants during the Second World War when people had more time than money. We belonged to a seed exchange with members all over the country. I was never much of a seed sower or gatherer, but I did manage to save some seed that other members wanted, and I reaped a harvest in correspondence. At that time Mrs. Knock was living in Crooks, South Dakota, but by taking things up in the fall, wintering them indoors, and putting them out again in the spring, she grew many things that in the North Carolina piedmont can be left in the garden all through the year.

"All my tender bulbs are in the garden now," she wrote me one June. "I set them out on the eighteenth of May. I have more than fifty amaryllis hybrids, white ismene, achimenes, chlidanthus, lachenalia, sprekelia, and three pots of *Vallota speciosa*. Do you care to exchange for any of the above? If so let me know." I sent her some *Zephyranthes candida*, and she sent me a vallota. The vallota went into the ground and that was the end of it. I don't know how the zephyranthes fared, for there was a gap in our correspondence when I moved from Raleigh to Charlotte. Then I came across some articles about passion flowers that Mrs. Knock published in *Flower and Garden*, and I wrote her through the magazine. She had, it turned out, moved to Minneapolis from Crooks. "Spring has arrived here," she answered me,

> but it keeps so cool, especially at night, with temperatures a little below freezing, that nothing is growing fast. Crocuses are blooming and the early forget-me-nots. That is all. But most perennials are coming up, and the primroses are in bud. My husband loves to garden. He has already raked and spaded, here and there where I will put in plants when we get frost-free nights. This time of year all the house plants are so anxious to get outside for the summer, and I am just as anxious to get away from all their muss and care. It takes three gallons of water to water all the pots in the windows and the glassed-in porch. The porch is our dining room all summer, and from it we get a good view of the whole backyard and its flowers and vegetables and fruit. We have raspberries, Concord grapes, apples, and plums. Our rhubarb

will soon be large enough to use, and it is so red and
pretty and delicious.

Mrs. Knock has written a book, *Passifloras for Your Garden*, about her collection of passionflowers grown from
seed sent to her from Hawaii, Jamaica, New Zealand, the
Canal Zone, South Africa, and various parts of this country.
She says *Passiflora caerulea* has survived temperatures of
twenty below zero when planted on the south or east
wall of a house and that *P. violacea* is even hardier. The
small-flowered passion vines bloom from seed the first
year and can be grown as annuals, but the others take
longer, and Mrs. Knock pots them up about two weeks
before frost and keeps them indoors until after the middle of May. When plants are left in the garden over winter,
it is well to take cuttings in the fall in order to have re-
placements if they are killed.

At the Hi-Mountain Farm in Seligman, Missouri, Ruth
Mooney grows native violets and wildflowers from the
Ozark Mountains. The violet collection is extensive and
includes several kinds not found in books, including *Viola
ozarkanum*, a rarity with scanty, small leaves and large blue
flowers with white centers. Miss Mooney lists three species of wild indigo that are seldom sold. *Baptisia leucophaea*
(which closely resembles *B. bracteata*) is a delightful rock
plant with large creamy flowers in drooping spikes that
used to bloom in my Raleigh garden around the first of
May. It has a wide range, from Michigan to Texas and
eastward to Georgia and South Carolina, and is available
from the Prarie Nursery. *B. leucantha* is somewhat taller,
with lovely upright spikes of pearl white flowers. It blooms
with me in early June and lasts for about two weeks. And

B. *vespertina* (vespertina in this case meaning western) is native to the plains and prairies from Kansas to Texas. A dwarf plant with blue flowers, it does well with regular watering and good soil, but may never bloom if it receives only the moisture that heaven sends.

In reading *Ozark Gardens* I like following the seasons in other parts of the country—spring in Texas, in Minnesota, in California. In one March issue, Madalene Modic wrote about her rock garden in Sewickley, Pennsylvania:

> The nice warm days in January and February found me outside looking over my rock garden. I had my bucket of soil, and I tucked in plants that had pushed out of the ground. I noticed the leaves of the cyclamen I had planted at the foot of a rhododendron, so pretty and green with their veined markings. Erica Snow Queen is full of tiny white bells and will be pretty for a long time. And now there's a new snowfall, which the rock garden plants will enjoy as the temperature falls to 15 tonight.

Ozark Gardens frequently carries articles about wildflowers. There's a regular column called "The Herb Corner." A page is devoted to cacti, and a special section in the classified pages is set aside for advertisements for them. The editor, Miss Bestard, conducts a "Bureau of Missing Plants," and all through the paper she makes editorial comments such as "Do order some plants from her," or "See advertisement" (inasmuch as the contributors are often advertisers as well). It is all very folksy, and full of firsthand knowledge about plants and gardens.

In every issue I find something of particular interest to

me. In one I read that Lola Massey wanted to swap *The Little Bulbs* by Elizabeth Lawrence for "bulbs of any sort which do not have to be lifted each fall." I sent her six magic lilies and rescued my book.

Small Blessings

Love, Mrs. Fergusson

When Mrs. George Fergusson's advertisement appeared in an issue of the Georgia bulletin, asking if anyone could help her find some redshank to help a friend, I wrote her and asked her to describe the plant she meant. Redshank (or shanks) is one of those common names shared by several plants, among them *Geranium robertianum*, *Rumex acetosa*, various species of polygonum, and others. "I'm old (nearly seventy)," Mrs. Fergusson wrote back, "and I can't remember how the plant looked." She said she wanted it for a friend who had stomach ulcers, and she related a bit of her own medical history, as regards what redshank had done for her.

In 1930 Mrs. Fergusson had pellagra. She weighed ninety pounds and was living on milk. She couldn't take the shots that the doctors were giving at the time, since they put her out for an hour and she had a baby to tend to. One day an Indian of the Cherokee tribe came driving up to her house. He told her that redshank would cure pellagra and stomach troubles, and asked her if she would try it. She said she would if she only knew what it was. Her daddy knew, and he went right out and dug a sack of roots. She drank redshank tea all that spring and summer, and by fall she weighed a hundred and forty pounds and could eat beans or onions or anything she wanted.

After she wrote to me, I sent Mrs. Fergusson a piece of sorrel and asked her whether it was the source of the pellagra medicine.

"Dear Friend," she replied.

> Received your letter with the leaf. No, red shank is a shrub herb, and don't have leaves like your leaf, but my friend, Mrs. Kerr, that I wanted it for, ordered a red shank plant from a man who answered my ad, and I think it's really the right thing. I am sure it is red shank for I chewed a limb from the plant and it is bitter. I still remember how bitter that tea was, but it was a grand medicine, and done lots for me. I believe it will cure my friend's stomach ulcers. She set out the plant she got. It has some leaves and good roots, and if it puts out leaves in the spring then we can dig some of the roots.

Mrs. Fergusson sent me one leaf. It was small and dark and oval. I sent it on to a friend in Birmingham, who was sure it was the New Jersey tea (*Ceanothus americanus*). I also ordered a shrub from the address Mrs. Fergusson gave me for the place her friend got her redshank—The Old Fashion Nursery in Boaz, Alabama. They sent me a shrub, with a letter from Mrs. Old Fashion, who wrote:

Dear Lady, I don't know what places this red shank grows. I have always lived in this state. My father and mother were strong believers in herb medicines. Red shank was used when someone was believed to have pellagra. Boil roots, drink one half cup of tea—also used for sore mouth. I also have blue grass, used for a laxative, life-everlasting, used for colds and flu, yellow root used for stomach ulcers, queen of meadow for kidney medicine, heart leaf for the heart. Wish I could find a market for the roots and herbs—many, many that I have and know.

Mrs. Fergusson raises hogs too, I learned from another of her advertisements in the Georgia bulletin: "Registered SPC hogs, service boars, bred sow, shoaty size boars, gilts; will have more pigs in May. All reasonably priced; see at lot near McCords Cross Road, Alabama. Place order in advance."

I wrote her about her hogs, and she wrote right back. "Yes, about the hogs," she wrote, "I have one sow with eight new pigs. She had nine but mashed one. Got one sow due this week. I have the best bloodlines in the registered Spotted Poland China, the long, lean meat type. Please tell your friends who may need breeding stock."

"You ask about flowers and garden," she went on. "I don't try to have many flowers since I got old, but do have a garden every year. I am getting too disabled to work much. I have heart trouble, high blood, and arthritis, so can't do much."

Mrs. Fergusson is a widow who lives alone on a farm in Cherokee County, Alabama, close to the Georgia border. Although she lives in the country, her house is fixed like the city: gas heat, indoor bath, TV. She invited me to pay her a visit, and I wish very much that I could. "Be sure to write again," her letter said. "I am a friend to all. Write me about yourself, a letter helps a lonely person. Love, Mrs. Fergusson."

Signs—and Prayers

Along with faith in herbal medicines, the bulletins evidence a lingering belief in planting by the signs. A friend who was brought up in the country told me that his grandfather always planted corn when the moon was low in the evening sky, so that the stalks would be low, and the strength would go to the ears, making them large and full. If seeds were sown when the moon is overhead, the stalk grows tall but the ears are poor. I was reminded of a passage in the *Georgics*. "If for harvest of wheat you ply the ground, and if grain alone is your aim, first let the daughters of Atlas [the Pleiades] pass from your sight in the morn, and let the Cretan star of the blazing crown withdraw ere you commit to the furrows the seed due, or hasten to trust the year's hope to a reluctant soil. Many have begun ere Maia's setting, but the looked-for crop has mocked them with empty ears."

One of my market bulletin friends who had asked for some cuttings told me to send them at the end of the month. "I always try to never sow seeds," she explained, "or set out plants or cuttings when the Zodiac signs are in the breast, and until after they pass down below the heart. You can laugh at me if you wish, but I have noticed that nothing ever does any good in that part of the signs. Do you ever notice the signs any?"

I had to go to *Blum's Farmer's and Planter's Almanac* to get this business clear in my mind. In it there is a diagram of the signs of the Zodiac arranged clockwise around the human figure with the ram overhead and the fishes underfoot, Cancer on the left side of the breast, and Leo on the opposite side at the heart. "Aries, Taurus, Libra, and Capricorn are good Fruitful Signs," Blum says. "Cancer, Scorpio, and Pisces are the best and most productive in the order named—being watery, they assist vegetation to withstand drought and produce much fruit and grain. Sagittarius and Aquarius are poor Signs. Leo, Gemini, and Virgo are Barren." My family's cook always planted a beautiful vegetable garden when I was a child, and I remember her saying, "Don't plant nothing under them twins." She always went by the almanac, and she never would plant parsley. "Sow parsley, sow trouble," she said.

I learned about Blum from Belle Clinton King, who says she had her first garden when she was five and has been planting flowers and vegetables for more than sixty years. She lives in Charlotte now, but she was reared on a farm. She is glad of that, she says, for out there she learned the essential things of life. She got up before daylight to milk the cows before going to school. When she was nine, no one else tended the cows, and now no one else puts a hoe to her vegetables. She does her own ditching with a lady spade and cuts the weeds with a power mower. And she plants by the signs. She plants her seed in the Cancer sign, all except cucumbers, which do well in Gemini.

Mrs. King always says a prayer before planting, and this too is another old custom.

"Not in vain do we watch the signs as they rise and

set," Virgil told the Roman farmers. "Mark the months and the signs of heaven. . . . Above all, worship the gods."

"Whensoever ye shall plant," a sixteenth-century gardener wrote, "it shall be meet and good for you to say as followeth: In the name of God the Father, the Sonne, and the holy Ghost, Amen. Increase and multiplye, and replenish the earth."

Chinaberries—and Mrs. Stowe

I don't recall ever seeing Chinaberry trees advertised in any of the market bulletins, and for good reason. Like the ailanthus and the paulownia, trees with which it has much in common, it just comes up, pretty much of its own accord, without human help to plant it. Nowadays, the Chinaberry tree grows in slums and alleys and run-down farm yards where it endures heat and drought and poor soil and thrives on abuse and neglect. But it was once called pride of India, and was considered a very fine thing. The Persians called this tree, botanically *Melia azedarach*, the "noble tree," and from their word for it comes the species name. A member of the mahogany family, this Asian plant is also called pride of China, Syrian bead tree, Japanese bead tree, and paradise tree. In England, where it has been grown ever since the middle of the sixteenth century or thereabouts, it is considered worthy of a place against the shelter of a wall, in the counties where it is hardy enough to grow out of doors. It grows in southern Italy, in Dalmatia, and all along the French Riviera, where many people treasure it for its grace and beauty of foliage and blossom. The small, fragrant, lilac flowers are borne in large loose clusters in April, and the leaves are twice pinnate, with slender tapered leaflets.

The translucent pale yellow berries hang on all winter. They are sought by birds and children and monks. The birds eat them, and the children and monks string the ivory seeds for necklaces and rosaries. When I was a child we dyed the seeds a dull rose color by soaking them in some horrible, ill-smelling liquid. Chinaberries still seem to have a fascination for children, which can be dangerous. The pulp is highly toxic; a friend of mine whose son ate just one fruit when he was a year old was advised by his pediatrician to take the child to the emergency room immediately to have his stomach pumped.

The Chinaberry is a small tree, to thirty or forty feet tall, open and graceful in habit and variable in form. The kind commonly grown is the Texas umbrella tree, *Melia azedarach umbraculiformis*, a variant form said to have originated on the battle field of San Jacinto. A friend in New Orleans calls this form the rain tree.

In spite of its charm and usefulness and the fact that it is not subject to disease or likely to be attacked by insects, the Chinaberry has its drawbacks. It is a dirty tree, littering the ground with fruit, leaves, and twigs, and although it grows very fast it is not long lived.

Chinaberries are hardy as far north as Virginia, and have been planted in the South since Colonial times. At Monticello Thomas Jefferson planted a grove on the southwest side of the roundabout, and it also grew in the gardens of Williamsburg. Before the Civil War it had become as typical of the South as lilacs are of New England. Longfellow wrote in "Evangeline" of the houses of planters shaded by China trees, and Harriet Beecher Stowe described them in detail. When Uncle Tom arrived at Simon Legree's plantation, "The wagon rolled up a weedy gravel walk, under a noble avenue of China trees, whose graceful forms and ever-springing foliage seemed to be the only things that neglect could not daunt or alter—like noble spirits, so deeply rooted in goodness, as to flourish and grow stronger amid discouragement and decay." And when Legree rode around the quarters on a moonlit night, "the shadows of the graceful China trees lay minutely pencilled on the turf below, and there was that transparent stillness in the air which it seemed almost unholy to disturb."

In *Uncle Tom's Cabin*, there are nice descriptions of gardens, not just of Chinaberry trees, as Mrs. Stowe contrasts the cool New England village that Miss Ophelia came from, with the semitropical brilliance of New Orleans. Her father's large farmhouse with "its clean-swept grassy yard, shaded by the dense and massive foliage of the sugar maple, had an air of order and stillness, of perpetuity and unchanging repose." And there were lilac bushes under the windows. When she reached New Orleans, her cousin's carriage drove through an arched gateway into a Moorish courtyard paved with a mosaic of pebbles. In the middle of the courtyard a fountain cast its silver water high in the air and let it splash on a border of sweet violets. "Two large orange trees, now fragrant with blossoms, threw a delicious shade; and ranged in a circle upon the turf were marble vases of the choicest flowering plants of the tropics. Huge pomegranate trees, with their glossy leaves and flame-colored flowers, dark-leaved Arabian jessamines with their silvery stars, geraniums, roses, lemon-scented verbena, all united with their bloom and fragrance."

"My own darling home!" Eva said. "Isn't it beautiful?"

And Miss Ophelia said as she alighted, "T'is a pretty place, though it looks rather old and heathenish to me."

The Thoreau Wildgarden

In a little bimonthly called *Backwoods Journal*, published at Paradox, New York, in the Adirondacks, I found an advertisement for The Thoreau Wildgarden and sent for its list of "native plants and green herbs." The nursery is near Concord, at the edge of the Easterbrook country, which Thoreau mentions in his *Journals*: "What a wild and rich domain that Easterbrook country!" He says in *Autumn*, "Not a cultivated, hardly a cultivable field in it, and yet it delights all natural persons, and feeds more still. Such great rocky and moist tracts . . . miles of huckleberries, and of barberries, and of wild apples, so fair both in flower and fruit. . . . I walk for two or three miles, and still the clumps of barberries, great sheaves with their wreaths of scarlet fruit, show themselves before me and on every side."

The old Carlisle road in the Easterbrook country was a road for "berry-pickers and no more worldly travelers." It was a road for walkers, Thoreau says, because the rocks and ruts would make rough riding in a wagon. It was "a road which leaves towns behind; where you put off worldly thoughts; where you do not carry a watch." As he made his way along it, on a September afternoon in 1859, he noticed the grateful scent of Dicksonia, the native hay-scented fern, (*Dennstaedtia punctilobula*). At this season, "Nature perfumes her garments with this essence. She gives it to those who go a-barberrying and on dank autumnal walks." When the leaves of other plants are down, the lingering greenness of the Dicksonia is more noticeable. The fronds "affect us as if they were evergreen, such persistant life and greenness in the midst of decay. No matter how much they are strewn with withered leaves, moist and green they spring above them, not fearing the frosts, fragile as they are. Their greenness is so much more interesting, because so many have already fallen, and we know that the first severe frost will cut them off too. In the summer greenness is cheap, now it is a thing comparatively rare, and is the emblem of life to us."

According to the list I sent for, The Thoreau Wildgarden has "a wild and woodsy appearance, in keeping with Thoreau's philosophy of simplicity." Boneset, tansy, and Joe-Pye-weed grow and seed themselves among the New England wildflowers, and in autumn Dicksonia scents the air. I like to think of these little gardens, all over the country, where simples and old-fashioned flowers, and even roadside weeds, are still treasured by those who garden for love.

Sources

In her revision of *A Southern Garden*, Elizabeth Lawrence remarked that some very choice and wonderful plants were almost impossible to find, but that there was pleasure nonetheless in seeking them out, even if the search was destined to end in failure. Readers of *Gardening for Love* will, I have no doubt whatever, be determined that they simply must have sky-highs or some rare crinum or other and many another plant besides, and then face the task of locating them, sometimes with unhappy outcome. To aid them in the search, I have assembled a list of nurseries whose catalogs offer "choice, rare, and unusual plants," as the heading reads on a useful list put together in late 1983 by Professor J. C. Raulston and M. K. Ramm of The N. C. State University Arboretum, from which I have freely borrowed, with some additions of my own. The Arboretum itself may in time introduce into the nursery trade some of the plants that came from Lawrence's garden. I have not annotated the list of nurseries since many of them are small, often run by one person, and the lists may vary from year to year. Catalog prices also date quickly. A self-addressed, stamped envelope enclosed with a request for catalog or plant will help the nursery provide information.

A. L.

Alpines West, Rt. 2, Box 259, Spokane, WA 99207

The Banana Tree, 715 Northampton St., Easton, PA 18042

B & D Lilies, Dept. H., 330 P St., Port Townsend, WA 98368

Bill Dodd's Rare Plants, P.O. Drawer 377, Semmes, AL 36575

Borbeleta Gardens, 10078 154th Ave., Elk River, MN 55330

Botanicals, 2791 S.E. 27th Ave., Gainesville, FL 32601

Camellia Forest Nursery, P.O. Box 291, Chapel Hill, NC 27514

Canyon Creek Nursery, 3527 Dry Creek Road, Oroville, CA 95965

Carroll Gardens, 444 East Main St., Westminster, MD 21157

The Country Garden, Rt. 2, Box 455A, Crivitz, WI 54414

Country Hills Greenhouse, Rt. 2, Corning, OH 43730

Crownsville Nursery, 1241 Generals Highway, Crownsville, MD 21032

C. A. Cruickshank, Ltd., 1015 Mt. Pleasant Road, Toronto, Ontario, Canada M4P 2M1

Daffodil Mart, Rt. 3, Box 208R, Glouster, VA 23061

Far North Gardens, 16785 Harrison, Livonia, MI 48154

Forestfarm, 990 Tetherhod, Williams, OR 97544

The Fragrant Path, P.O. Box 328, Fort Calhoun, NE 68023

Gladside Gardens, Northfield, MA 01360

The Glass House Works Greenhouse, Church St., Box 97, Stewart, OH 45778-0097

Gossler Farms Nursery, 1200 Weaver Road, Springfield, OR 97473

Russell Graham, 4030 Eagle Crest Rd. NW, Salem, OR 97304

Green Horizons, 500 Thompson, Kerrville, TX 78028

Hidden Springs Nursery, Rt. 14, Box 159, Cookeville, TN 38501

High Country Rosarian, 1717 Downing St., Denver, CO 80218

Holbrook Farm and Nursery, Rt. 2, Box 223B, Fletcher, NC 28732

J. L. Hudson, Seedsman, Box 1058H, Redwood City, CA 94064

Klaus R. Jelitto, Postfach 560 127, D-2000 Hamburg 56, West Germany

J. W. Jung Seed Co., Box B-28, Randolph, WI 53957

Lamb Nurseries, E. 101 Sharp Ave., Spokane, WA 99202

Logee's Greenhouse, Dept. H, 55 North St., Danielson, CT 06239

Louisiana Nursery, Rt. 7, Box 43, Opelousas, LA 70570

John Lyon's, Inc., 143 Alewife Brook Parkway, Cambridge, MA 02140

McClure & Zimmerman, 1422 Thorndale, Chicago, IL 60660

Merry Gardens, Camden, ME 04843

Mid-Atlantic Wildflowers, S/R Box 226, Gloucester Point, VA 23062

Montrose Nursery, P.O. Box 957, Hillsborough, NC 27278

Nature's Garden, Rt. 1, Box 488, Beaverton, OR 97007

Niche Gardens, Rt. 1, Box 290, Chapel Hill, NC 27514

Nichols Garden Nursery, 1190 North Pacific Hwy, Albany, OR 97321

Park Seed Co., Inc., S.C. Highway 254N., Greenwood, SC 29647

Prarie Nursery, P.O. Box 365, Westfield, WI 53964

Primrose Path, RD 1, Box 78, Scottdale, PA 15683

Salter Tree Farm, Rt. 2, Box 1332, Madison, FL 32340

The Sandy Mush Herb Nursery, Rt. 2, Surret Cove Rd., Leicester, NC 28748

John Scheepers, Inc., 63 Wall St., New York, NY 10005

Shady Lawn Nursery, 637 Holly Lane, Plantation, FL 33317

Shield Horticultural Gardens, Box 92, Westerfield, IN 46074

Siskiyou Rare Plant Nursery, 2825 Cummings Rd., Medford, OR 97501

Stallings Nursery, 910-H Encinitas Blvd., Encinitas, CA 92024

Sweet Springs Perennial Growers, 2065 Ferndale Rd., P.O. Box 1315, Arroyo Grande, CA 93420

Thomasville Nurseries, Inc., P.O. Box 7, Thomasville, GA 31792

Thompson and Morgan, Inc., Dept. H.C., P.O. Box 1308, Jackson, NJ 08527

Tyty Plantation, Box 159, Tyty, GA 31795

Andre Viette Farm and Nursery, Rt. 1, Box 16, Fishersville, VA 22939

Mary Walker Bulb Co., Box 256, Omega, GA 31775

We-Du Nurseries, Rt. 5, Box 724, Marion, NC 28752

Willetts, P.O. Box 446, Fremont, CA 94536

Woodlanders, 1128 Colleton Ave., Aiken, SC 29801

Market Bulletins

Alabama Market Bulletin, 1455 Federal Drive, P.O. Box 3336, Montgomery, AL 36193. Subscription, $2.50 a year. (205) 261-5872.

Arkansas State Plant Board News, Box 1069, Little Rock, AR 72203. (501) 225-1598.

Connecticut Forward Thinking Agriculture, State Office Building, Hartford, CT 06106. (203) 566-4276.

Florida Market Bulletin, Florida Department of Agriculture and Consumer Services, Mayo Building, 407 South Calhoun Street, Tallahassee, FL 32301. Subscription, $3.00 a year. (904) 488-4211.

Georgia Farmers and Consumers Market Bulletin, State Department of Agriculture, 19 Martin Luther King, Jr., Drive SW, Atlanta, GA 30334

Hawaii's AG Notes, Public Information Office, 1428 South King Street, Honolulu, HI 96814. (808) 548-7109.

Indiana AG Notes, Indiana Department of Commerce, Division of Agriculture, 1 North Capitol, Suite 700, Indianapolis, IN 46204-2288. (317) 232-8770.

Kentucky Agricultural News, 722 Capital Plaza Tower, Frankfort, KY 40601. (502) 564-3394.

Mississippi Market Bulletin, P.O. Box 1118, Jackson, MS 39205. Subscription, $5.00 a year. (601) 359-3657.

Weekly Market Bulletin, New Hampshire Department of Agriculture, Concord Center, 10 Ferry Street, Concord, NH 03301. Subscription, $10.00 a year. (603) 271-2505.

North Carolina Agricultural Review, P.O. Box 27647, Raleigh, NC 27611. (919) 733-4216.

Agricultural News Bulletin, Pennsylvania Department of Agriculture, 2301 North Cameron Street, Harrisburg, PA 17110-9408. (717) 787-5085.

South Carolina Market Bulletin, South Carolina Department of Agriculture, Wade Hampton State Office Building, Columbia, SC 29201. (803) 758-2426.

The Gleanings, South Dakota Department of Agriculture, 445 East Capitol, Pierre, SD 57501. (605) 224-1343.

Tennessee Agri-Report, Tennessee Department of Agriculture, Ellington Agricultural Center, Box 40627, Melrose Station, Nashville, TN 37204. (615) 360-0117.

Tennessee Farm Bureau News, P.O. Box 313, Columbia, TN 38402-0313.

Texas Gazette, Texas Department of Agriculture, P.O. Box 12847, Austin, TX 78711. (512) 463-7593.

West Virginia Market Bulletin, West Virginia Department of Agriculture, State Capitol, Charleston, WV 25305. (304) 348-3798.

List of Common Plant Names

Note. The standard source for common and folk names of plants grown in the United States is an index in Hortus Third, a reference Elizabeth Lawrence used constantly. Many of the common names she encountered in the market bulletins appear in Hortus as well, but some do not, being local or regional names, often names peculiar to the South, in many cases with a long history and tradition behind them. For readers who share Lawrence's interest in common names, the following list, keyed to botanical or scientific names, is provided. (A. L.)

Adam-and-Eve root: *Aplectrum hyemale*
Adder's violet: *Goodyera pubescens*
Ague root: *Aletris farinosa*
Ague-weed: *Gentiana andrewsii*
Air potato: *Dioscorea bulbifera*
Alehoof: *Glechoma hederacea*
Aluminum plant: *Pilea cadierei*
Alumroot: *Heuchera americana*
Angelica root: *Angelica atropurpurea*
Angel lily: *Crinum*
Angel trumpet: *Datura*
Anise tree: *Illicium floridanum*
Apostle lily: *Crinum*

Bachelor's buttons: *Gomphrena globosa*
Baptist plant: *Alternanthera ficoidea* 'Bettzickiana'
Bead seeds: *Coix lacryma-jobi*
Bee balm: *Monarda didyma*
Bird-of-Paradise: *Caesalpinia gilliesii; Strelitzia reginae*
Bird's-eye-bush: *Symphoricarpos orbiculatus*
Bishop's weed: *Aegopodium podagraria*
Blackberry lily: *Belamcanda chinensis*
Blackberry rose: *Rubus coronarius*
Black-eyed susan: *Rudbeckia hirta; Thunbergia alata*
Black-heart: *Epilobium angustifolius*
Black snakeroot: *Aristolochia serpentaria; Cimicifuga racemosa*
Blazing star: *Liatris spicata*
Bleeding petunia: *Achimenes*
Bloodroot: *Sanguinaria canadensis*
Bloody mary: *Lychnis coronaria*
Bloody william: *Lychnis coronaria*
Blooming sally: *Epilobium angustifolium*
Blue bottles: *Muscari*
Blue cohosh: *Caulophyllum thalictroides*
Blue jugs: *Muscari*
Bocconia: *Macleaya cordata*
Bois d'arc: *Maclura pomifera*
Bonaparte's crown: *Euphorbia cyparissias*
Bouncing bet: *Saponaria officinalis*
Bowing-lady: *Clerodendrum indicum*
Brazilian coral tree: *Erythrina crista-galli*
Brazilian-plume: *Justicia carnea*
Bridal rose: *Rubus coronarius*
Bride bouquet: *Saponaria officinalis*
Brideflower: *Achillea ptarmica*
Burning bush: *Euonymus americana; Chaenomeles*
Bursting heart: *Euonymus americana*
Butcher's broom: *Ruscus aculeatus angustifolius*
Butter-and-eggs: *Linaria vulgaris*
Butterfly lily: *Hedychium coronarium*
Butterfly weed: *Asclepias tuberosa*
Button snakeroot: *Liatris spicata*

Cabbage rose: *Rosa centifolia*
Calico border plant: *Achillea millefolium*
Canada violet: *Viola canadensis*
Canary tree: *Cassia corymbosa*
Candleberry tree: *Sapium sebiferum*
Candlestick lily, candystick lily: *Crinum scabrum*
Candy roaster, candy rooster: edible melon or pumpkin seeds, roasted
Carnation rose: *Rubus coronarius*
Carolina allspice: *Calycanthus floridus*
Cashmere bouquet: *Clerodendrum philippinum*
Cassabanana vine: *Sicana odorifera*
Cat-bell: *Crotalaria sagittalis*
Cat's paw: *Hepatica*
Century plant: *Agave americana*
Chenille plant: *Acalypha hispida*
Chicken gizzard: *Iresine herbstii*
Chinaberry: *Melia azedarach*
Chinese bottle tree: *Firmiana simplex*
Chinese hollyhock: *Malva sylvestris*
Chinese parasol tree: *Firmiana simplex*
Chinese tallow tree: *Sapium sebiferum*
Chocolate vine: *Akebia quinata*
Christ-in-a-hamper: *Rhoeo spathacea*
Chufa: *Cyperus esculentus sativus*
Citronella: *Collinsonia canadensis*
Climbing hibiscus: *Hibiscus radiatus* 'flore-pleno'
Climbing okra: *Luffa*
Clock vine: *Thunbergia alata*
Cocklebur: *Agrimonia eupatoria*
Colic root: *Aletris farinosa*
Coneflower: *Echinacea*
Confederate jessamine: *Trachelospermum jasminoides*
Confederate lily: *Crinum fimbriatulum*
Confederate rose: *Hibiscus mutabilis*
Congo root: *Psoralea psoraliodes*
Coon root: *Sanguinaria canadensis*
Coral bean: *Erythrina herbacea*
Coral berry: *Symphoricarpos orbiculatus*

Coral vine: *Antigonon leptopus*
Corkscrew: *Vigna caracalla*
Cow-itch: *Campsis radicans*
Creasy: *Barbarea vulgaris*
Creeping charlie: *Glechoma hederacea*
Creeping verbena: *Calystegia hederacea*
Creole box: *Buxus microphylla japonica*
Cross vine: *Bignonia capreolata*
Cruel vine: *Araujia sericifera*
Crybaby: *Erythrina crista-galli*
Cuckoo's bread: *Plantago major*
Cucumber tree: *Magnolia acuminata*

Damask rose: *Rosa centifolia*
Devil's backbone: *Pedilanthus tithymaloides*
Devil's bone: *Pedilanthus tithymaloides*
Devil's nip: Jack-in-the-pulpit; *Arisaema triphyllum*
Devil's pincushion: *Leonotis nepetifolia*
Devil's shoestring: *Yucca filamentosa*
Devil's walking stick: *Aralia spinosa*
Dewdrop: *Leucojum aestivum*
Dog rose: *Rosa canina*
Downy rattlesnake plantain: *Goodyera pubescens*

Earth almond: *Cyperus esculentus sativus*
Earth nut: *Cyperus esculentus sativus*
Ear tree: *Enterolobium*
Easter rose: *Rubus coronarius*
Eleven-o'clock lady: *Ornithogalum umbellatum*
English dogwood: *Philadelphus*

Fairy lily: *Zephyranthes*
False dragon: *Physostegia virginiana*
Feather hyacinth: *Muscari comosum* 'Plumosum'
Firecracker plant: *Monarda didyma*
Firecracker vine: *Manettia inflata*
Fireweed: *Epilobium angustifolium*
Fish-bait tree: *Catalpa*

Flaming fountain: *Amaranthus tricolor salicifolius*
Flower-of-death: *Vinca minor*
Fortune grass: *Pennisetum setaceum*
Fountain grass: *Pennisetum setaceum*

Gall-flower: *Gentiana andrewsii*
Gill-go-over-the-ground: *Glechoma hederacea*
Ginger lily: *Hedychium coronarium*
Ginseng: *Panax quinquefolius*
Golden dewdrop: *Duranta repens*
Goldenrain tree: *Koelreuteria paniculata; K. bipinnata*
Goldenseal: *Hydrastis canadensis*
Goodbye-summer: *Saponaria officinalis*
Good-morning-spring: *Claytonia virginica*
Grandfather's whiskers: *Cleome*
Grass lily: *Ornithogalum umbellatum*
Grass nut: *Cyperus esculentus sativus*
Graveyard moss: *Euphorbia cyparissias; Sedum sarmentosum*
Graveyard vine: *Vinca minor*
Ground ivy: *Glechoma hederacea*

Halberd-leaved violet: *Viola hastata*
Hardy orange: *Poncirus trifoliata*
Haymaids: *Glechoma hederacea*
Hay-scented fern: *Dennstaedtia punctilobula*
Heal-all: *Collinsonia canadensis; Prunella vulgaris*
Heart-bursting-with-love: *Euonymus americana*
Hedgemaids: *Glechoma hederacea*
Hidden lily: *Curcuma petiolata*
Hop hornbeam: *Ostrya virginiana*
Hummingbird plant: *Spirea × bumalda* 'Anthony Waterer'

Ice-apple: *Symphoricarpos albus*
Indian bead: *Coix lacryma-jobi*
Indian currant: *Symphoricarpos orbiculatus*

Jacob's ladder: *Gladiolus byzantinus*
Japanese bead tree: *Melia azedarach*

Japanese golden eggs: *Solanum integrifolium*
Japanese varnish tree: *Firmiana simplex*
Jewels of Opar: *Talinum paniculatum*
Job's tears: *Coix lacryma-jobi*
Joseph's coat: *Alternanthera ficoides* 'Bettzickiana'
Joy-of-the-ground: *Vinca minor*
June bell: *Campanula rapunculoides*
Juno's tears: *Coix lacryma-jobi*

King flower: *Echinacea purpurea*
Kiss-me-and-I'll-tell-you: *Buddleia*
Kiss-me-at-the-garden-gate: *Polygonum orientale*
Kiss-me-dick: *Euphorbia cyparissias*

Lady-at-the-gate: *Saponaria officinalis*
Ladyfingers: *Polygonum orientale*
Lady slipper: *Impatiens balsamina*
Lady's thumb: *Epilobium angustifolium*
Lemon balm: *Melissa officinalis*
Lemon cucumber: *Cucumis melo* Chito
Leverwood: *Ostrya virginiana*
Life-everlasting: *Gnaphalium obtusifolium*
London pride: *Lychnis chalcedonica; Saxifraga umbrosa*
Love apple: *Solanum integrifolium*
Love-in-a-tangle: *Selaginella uncinata*
Lover's-pride: *Epilobium angustifolium*

Mamou: *Erythrina herbacea*
Mandrake root: *Podophyllum peltatum*
Mango melon: *Cucumis melo* Chito
Man-in-boat: *Rhoeo spathacea*
Marble vine: *Diplocyclos palmatus*
Marsh clematis: *Clematis crispa*
May apple: *Podophyllum peltatum*
Meadow rue: *Thalictrum revolutum; T. polygamum*
Mexicali rose: *Clerodendrum bungei*
Mexican flame vine: *Senecio confusus*
Mexican hydrangea: *Clerodendrum bungei*

Milk-and-wine lily: *Crinum*
Mirliton: *Sechium edule*
Mole plant: *Euphorbia lathyris*
Monkey-face petunia, monkey-face plant: *Achimenes*
Moon lily: *Datura inoxia* subsp. *inoxia*
Moses-in-a-cradle, Moses-in-the-bullrushes, Moses-on-a-raft: *Rhoeo spathacea*
Moss acacia: *Robinia hispida*
Mother-in-law plant: *Dieffenbachia*
Mother-of-thousands: *Saxifraga stolonifera*
Mother's Day rose: *Rubus coronarius*
Mountain bluet: *Hedyotis purpurea*
Mountain dittany: *Cunila origanoides*
Mountain ebony: *Bauhinia variegata*
Mountain ivy, mountain laurel: *Kalmia*
Mountain lettuce: *Saxifraga micranthidifolia*
Mountain pink: *Phlox subulata*
Mountain spinach: *Atriplex hortensis*
Musk mallow: *Malva moschata*

Naked ladies: *Zephyranthes atamasco*
New Jersey tea: *Ceanothus americanus*
Nodding toad: *Trillium*
Nun's rose: *Rubus coronarius*

October pink: *Chrysanthemum*
Old maid: *Zinnia*
Orach: *Atriplex hortensis*
Orchid iris: *Iris virginica*
Orchid tree: *Bauhinia variegata*
Oriental rose: *Calystegia hederacea*
Osage orange: *Maclura pomifera*
Oxeye: *Buphthalum salicifolium*

Papooseroot: *Caulophyllum thalictroides*
Paradise tree: *Melia azedarach*
Partridgeberry: *Mitchella repens*
Passion vine: *Passiflora*

Peacock fern: *Selaginella uncinata*
Phoenix tree: *Firmiana simplex*
Pineapple lily: *Eucomis comosa*
Pine-bur begonia: *Justicia carnea*
Plantain: *Plantago major*
Plantation: *Plantago major*
Pleurisy root: *Asclepias tuberosa*
Plume plant: *Justicia carnea*
Plume poppy: *Macleaya cordata*
Poke root, poke salit, poke weed: *Phytolacca americana*
Polka-dot plant: *Hypoestes phyllostachya*
Pomegranate: *Cucumis melo* Dudaim; *Punica granatum*
Poor man's stephanotis: *Araujia sericifera*
Porch vine: *Clematis*
Potato vine: *Dioscorea bulbifera*
Pride of China: *Melia azedarach*
Pride of India: *Melia azedarach*
Prince's feather: *Saxifraga umbrosa*
Princess feather: *Polygonum orientale*
Prissy feather tree: lilac; *Syringia vulgaris*
Puccoon: *Sanguinaria canadensis*
Purple-nut sedge: *Cyperus rotundus*
Pussy ears: *Cyanotis somaliensis*

Queen Anne's pocket melon: *Cucumis melo* Dudaim
Queen's delight, queen's root: *Stillingia sylvatica*

Rabbit tobacco: *Gnaphalium obtusifolium*
Rainbow moss: *Selaginella uncinata*
Rain lily: *Zephyranthes*
Rain tree: *Melia azedarach* 'Umbraculiformis'; *Samanea saman*
Raisin vine: *Akebia quinata*
Redbird bush: *Fuchsia*
Redbird cactus: *Pedilanthus tithymaloides*
Red magnolia: *Illicium floridanum*
Redshank: *Ceanothus americanus*; *Geranium robertianum*; *Polygonum*; *Rumex acetosa*
Red snowberry: *Symphoricarpos orbiculatus*

Red wisteria: *Sesbania punicea*
Root of the Holy Ghost: *Angelica archangelica; A. atropurpurea*
Rosa de montana: *Antigonon leptopus*
Rose acacia: *Robinia hispida*
Rose-of-Sharon: *Hibiscus syriacus; Hypericum calcynium; Robinia hispida*
Rose-that-lives-forever: *Sedum spectabile*
Rover bellflower: *Campanula rapunculoides*
Roving sailor: *Saxifraga stolonifera*
Rubber plant: *Ficus elastica*

St. Joseph's lily: *Hippeastrum × johnsonii*
Salad burnet: *Poterium sanguisorba*
Sally-at-the-gate: *Saponaria officinalis*
Sampson's snakeroot: *Gentiana andrewsii; G. saponaria; G. villosa; Psoralea psoraliodes*
Sangrel snakeroot, sangrel snakeweed: *Aristolochia serpentaria*
Sanicle snakeroot: *Sanicula marilandica*
Seal: *Hydrastis canadensis*
Sea willow: *Amaranthus tricolor salicifolius*
Seneca snakeroot: *Polygala senega*
Seng: *Panax quinquefolius*
Sensitive brier, sensitive vine: *Schrankia microphylla; S. nuttallii*
Seven-years'-love: *Achillea ptarmica*
Shame vine: *Schrankia microphylla; S. nuttallii*
Shawneehaw: *Viburnum cassinoides*
Shawnee salad: *Hydrophyllum virginianum*
Shoemake: *Rhus*
Shrimp plant: *Justicia brandegeana*
Silk oak: *Grevillea robusta*
Silver-bell: *Halesia*
Silver-lace vine: *Polygonum aubertii*
Sky-high: *Hibiscus radiatus* cv. 'flore-pleno'
Snail flower: *Vigna caracalla*
Snakeroot: *Collinsonia canadensis*
Snowberry: *Symphoricarpos albus*
Snowdrop: *Leucojum aestivum; Galanthus nivalis*
Snowflake: *Leucojum aestivum; Galanthus nivalis*
Spider flower: *Cleome*

Spider legs: *Cleome*
Spider lily: *Lycoris squamigera; L. radiata*
Spider plant: *Chlorophytum*
Spiderwort: *Tradescantia virginiana*
Spindle tree: *Euonymus americana*
Spirit bean: *Erythrina herbacea*
Spring beauty: *Claytonia virginica*
Squawroot: *Mitchella repens*
Star of Bethlehem: *Ornithogalum umbellatum*
Star root: *Aletris farinosa*
Stonewort: *Collinsonia canadensis*
Strawberry-begonia: *Saxifraga stolonifera*
Strawberry bush: *Euonymus americana*
Strawberry-geranium: *Saxifraga stolonifera*
Sun wheel: *Buphthalum salicifolium*
Surprise lily: *Lycoris squamigera*
Swamp rose: *Rosa nitida*
Sweetbriar: *Rosa eglanteria*
Sweet shrub: *Calycanthus floridus*
Syrian bead tree: *Melia azedarach*

Texas umbrella tree: *Melia azedarach* 'Umbraculiformis'
Three-men-in-a-boat: *Rhoeo spathacea*
Thrift: *Armeria; Phlox subulata*
Toadflax: *Linaria vulgaris*
Toper's plant: *Poterium sanguisorba*
Torch flower: *Tithonia rotundifolia*
Trumpet vine: *Campsis radicans*
Turkeyberry: *Symphoricarpos orbiculatus*
Turkey-gobbler beads: *Symphoricarpos orbiculatus*
Twinberry: *Mitchella repens*

Unicorn root: *Aletris farinosa*

Venus flytrap: *Dionaea muscipula*
Vesper iris: *Pardanthopis dichotoma*
Vine peach: *Cucumis melo Dudaim*
Virginia rose: *Hibiscus mutabilis*

Virginia snakeroot: *Aristolochia serpentaria*

Wahoo: *Euonymus americana; E. atropurpurea; Ulmus elata*
Wall-pepper: *Sedum acre*
Waterleaf: *Hydrophyllum virginianum*
Waybread: *Plantago major*
Wedding bells: *Forsythia viridissima*
Welcome-home-husband-but-never-so-drunk: *Sedum acre*
Welcome-to-our-house: *Euphorbia cyparissias*
Whispering charlie: *Aegopodium podagraria*
Widow's tears: *Achimenes; Tradescantia*
Wild indigo: *Baptisia*
Wild peanut: *Erythronium*
Wild petunia: *Ruellia ciliosa*
Wild raisin: *Viburnum cassinoides*
Wild raspberry: *Rubus odoratus*
Wild sweet william: *Saponaria officinalis*
Winter cress: *Barbarea vulgaris*
Winter jasmine: *Jasminum nudiflorum*
Wishbone flower: *Torenia*
Witch elm: *Ulmus alata*
Withe-rod: *Viburnum cassinoides*
Wood rose: *Merremia tuberosa*

Yarrow: *Achillea millefolium*
Yellow bignonia: *Macfadyena unguis-cati*
Yellow-fringed orchid: *Habenaria ciliaris*
Yellow-nut sedge: *Cyperus esculentus*
Yellowroot: *Hydrastis canadensis*
Yellow rose of Texas: Harison's yellow rose; *Kerria japonica*

Bibliography

Bailey, Liberty Hyde. *The Garden of Gourds, with Decorations*. New York: Macmillan, 1937.

Ballard, Ernesta Drinker. *Garden in Your House*. New York: Harper and Row, 1971.

Bartolomaeus, Anglicus (13th century). *Mediaeval Lore from Bartolomaeus Anglicus*. By Robert Steele. Preface by William Morris. London: Chatow and Windus; Boston: Luce, 1907.

Bartram, William. *Travels through North and S. Carolina; Georgia, east and west Florida*. London, 1792. Reprint. Dover, 1955.

———. *An Account of the species, hybrids, & other varieties of the Vine of North America*. New York, 1804.

Beverley, Robert. *The History & Present State of Virginia . . . by a Native of the Place*. London, 1705. Reprint. Ed., with an intro., by Louis B. Wright. Chapel Hill: University of North Carolina Press, 1947.

Blum, L. V. *Blum's Farmer's and Planter's Almanac for the Year*. Salem, N.C.: Blum, 18—.

Bowles, E. A. *A Handbook of Crocus and Colchicums for Gardeners*. Toronto: Van Nostrand, 1952.

Brickell, John. *The Natural history of North Carolina, With and account of trade, manners, and customs of the Christian and Indian inhabitants*. Dublin, 1737. Reprint. New York: Johnson Reprint Corp., 1969.

Britton, Nathaniel Lord, and Hon. Addison Brown. *An Illustrated Flora of* the Northern United States, Canada and the British Possessions. . . . 3 vols. New York: New York Botanical Garden, 1943.

Burton, Robert. *Anatomy of Melancholy*. Oxford, 1621. Reprint. New York: Tudor, 1941.

Cobbett, William. *The American Gardener: Or a treatise on the situation, soil, fencing and laying-out of gardens, on the making and managing of hot-beds, and green-houses, and on the propagation and cultivation of all sorts of kitchen-garden plants*. . . . London: C. Clement, 1821.

Colette. "For a Flower Album." In Colette. *Flowers and Fruit*. Ed. Robert Phelps. Trans. Matthew Ward. New York: Farrar Straus and Giroux, 1985.

Collinson, Peter. "Brothers of the Spade: Correspondence of Peter Collinson of London & John Custis of Williamsburg Virginia." Proceedings of the American Antiquarian Society. Worcester, Mass. Vol. 58.

Culpeper, Nicholas. *Complete herbal and English physician wherein several hundred herbs are physically applied to the cure of all disorders incident to man, with rules for compounding them*. London: Thomas Kelly, 1653.

———. *Culpeper's Complete herbal*. Secaucus, N.J.: Chartwell Books, 1985.

Dykes, William Rickatson. *The Genus Iris*. Cambridge: Cambridge University Press, 1913. Reprint. New York: Dover, 1974.

Earle, Alice Morse. *Old Time Gardens*. New York: Macmillan, 1901. Detroit: Singing Tree Press, 1968.

Ellacombe, Canon. *In My Vicarage Garden and Elsewhere*. London: Edward Arnold, 1896.

Friend, Hilderic. *Flowers and Flower Lore*. London: G. Allen, (pre-1883). Reprint. Rockport, Mass.: Para Research, 1981.

Gerard, John. *The Herbal: Or General history of plantes*. London: 1596. Reprint of 2d ed. (London, 1633). New York, Dover, 1975.

———. *Leaves from Gerard's Herball*. Ed. Marcus Woodward. Boston: Houghton Mifflin, 1931. Reprint. New York: Dover, 1969.

Gibbons, Euell. *Stalking the Healthful Herbs*. New York: McKay, 1966.

Gleason, Henry Allan. *The New Britton & Brown Illustrated Flora of the N.E. United States and Adjacent Canada*. New York: New York Botanical Garden, 1952.

The Good Huswiues handmaid, for cookerie in her kitchin in dressing all maner of meat, with other wholsom diet, for her household. . . . London? R. Jones, 1588?. University Microfilms no. 11072.

Grabe, Andrebe Vilas. *Complete Book of House Plants.* New York: Random House, 1958.

Green, Ely. *An Autobiography.* New York: Seabury Press, 1966.

Grieve, Maud. *A Modern Herbal: The Medicinal, Culinary, Cosmetic, and Economic Properties, Cultivation and Folklore of Herbs and Grasses. . . .* Ed. Hilda Leyel. New York: Harcourt Brace, 1931. Reprint. New York: Dover, 1971.

Hearn, Lafcadio. *Creole Sketches.* Boston: Houghton Mifflin, 1928.

Hortus Third: A concise dictionary of plants, cultivated in the United States and Canada. Initially compiled by Liberty Hyde Bailey and Ethel Zoe Bailey. Rev. and exp. by staff of the Liberty Hyde Bailey Hortarium. New York: Macmillan, 1976.

Ingwersen, Will. *The Wisley Book of Gardening: A Guide for Enthusiasts.* Ed. Robert Pearson. New York: Norton, 1983.

———. *Ingwersen's Manual of Alpine Plants.* Eastbourne, U.K.: Dunnsprint, 1978.

———. *Classic Garden Plants.* Portland, Ore.: Timber Press, 1980.

Jefferson, Thomas. *Garden Book, 1766–1824, with relevant extracts from his other writings, annotated by Edwin Morris Betts.* Philadelphia: American Philosophical Society, 1944.

Jewett, Sarah Orne. *The Country of the Pointed Firs and Other Stories.* New York: Norton, 1982.

Josselyn, John. *New England's rarities discovered.* London: G. Widdowes, 1672. Reprint. Boston: W. Veasie, 1865; Berlin: W. Junk, 1926.

Justice, William S., and C. Ritchie Bell. *Wild Flowers of North Carolina.* Chapel Hill: University of North Carolina Press, 1968.

Kalm, Peter. *Travels into North America; containing its natural history, and a circumstantial account of its plantations and agriculture in general. . . .* London: T. Lowndes, 1772.

Knock, Florence. *Passifloras for Your Garden.* Kansas City: Diversity Books, 1965.

Loudon, Jane Webb. *Gardening for ladies; and Companion to the flower garden.* 1st American ed. New York: Wiley and Putnam, 1848.

Lounsberry, Alice. *Southern Wild Flowers and Trees.* New York: F. A. Stokes, 1901.

McKinney, Ella Porter. *Iris in the Little Garden.* Boston: Little, Brown. 1927.

Muenscher, Walter Conrad Leopold. *Poisonous Plants of the United States.* New York: Macmillan, 1939.

Nehrling, Henry. *The Plant World in Florida; from the published manuscripts of Dr. Henry Nehrling;* coll. and ed. Alfred and Elizabeth Kay. New York: Macmillan, 1933.

Paracelsus. *Selected Writings.* Trans. Norbert Guterman. New York: Pantheon, 1951.

Parkinson, John. *Paradisi in sole paradisus terrestris: or a garden of all sorts of pleasant flowers. . . .* London: Lownes and Young, 1629.

———. *A Garden of Pleasant Flowers.* Ed. Alfred Hyatt. New York: Dover, 1976.

Parson, Frances Theodora (Mrs. Dana). *How to Know the Wild Flowers; a guide to the names, haunts, and habits of our common wild flowers.* New York: Scribner's, 1896.

Pliny, the Elder (A.D. 23–79). *The History of the World, commonly called The natural history of C. Plinius Secundus, or Pliny.* New York: McGraw-Hill, 1964.

Porcher, Francis Peyre. *Report on the indigenous medicinal plants of South Carolina.* n.p., n.p., n.d.

———. *Resources of the southern fields and forests; medical, economical, and agricultural; being also a medical botany of the Confederate states; with practical information on the useful properties of the trees, plants, and shrubs.* Prepared and published by order of the Surgeon-General, Richmond, Va. Charleston: Evans and Cogswell, 1863.

Pratt, Anne. *The Flowering Plants, Grasses, Sedges, and Ferns of Great Britain.* 5 vols. London and New York: Warne, 1870.

Rohde, Eleanour Sinclaire. *The Scented Garden.* London: Medici Society, 1931.

———. *A Garden of Herbs.* London: Jenkins, 1926.

Shelton, Jane deForest. *The Salt-Box House: Eighteenth Century Life in the Hill Town.* New York: Baker & Taylor, 1900. Reprint. New York: Scribner's, 1929.

Streever, Fred. *The American Trail Hound.* Sportsman's Library Series. New York: A. S. Barnes, 1948.

Thoreau, Henry David. *Autumn and Winter: From the Journal of Henry D. Thoreau.* Boston: Houghton Mifflin, 1929.

Traub, Hamilton. *The Amaryllis Manual.* New York: Macmillan, 1958.

Venner, Tobias. *Via recta ad vitam longam: A plaine philosophicall demonstration of the nature, faculties, and affects of all such things as by way of nourishments*

make for the preservation of health. . . . Ann Arbor: University Microfilms, 1975.

Vick, James. *Flower and Vegetable Garden*. Rochester, N. Y.: J. Vick, 1878.

Virgil. *The Georgics*. Trans. L. P. Wilkinson. New York: Penguin, 1983.

Welty, Eudora. "The Golden Apples." In *The Collected Stories of Eudora
Welty*. New York and London: Harcourt Brace Jovanovich, 1980.

———. *Losing Battles*. New York: Random House, 1970.

Wilder, Louise Beebe. *The Fragrant Path: A Book about Sweet-Scented Flowers
and Leaves*. New York: Macmillan, 1932. Reprinted as *The Fragrant
Garden*. New York: Dover, 1974.

Wood, Alphonso. *Flora Atlantica: The American botanist and florist: Including
lessons in the structure, life, and growth of plants; together with a simple
analytical flora*. . . . New York and Chicago: A. S. Barnes, 1876.

Wood, George Bacon, and Franklin Bache. *The Dispensatory of the United
States of America*. 1st ed. Philadelphia: Grigg & Elliot, 1833. 23d ed.
Philadelphia: Lippincott, 1943.

Index